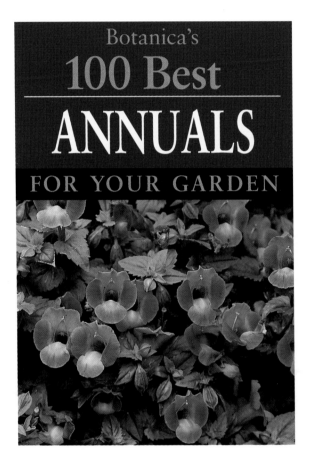

Botanica's
100 Best
ANNUALS
FOR YOUR GARDEN

Botanica's
100 Best
ANNUALS
FOR YOUR GARDEN

LAUREL
GLEN

First published in 2000 in North America by
Laurel Glen Publishing
An imprint of the Advantage Publishers Group
5880 Oberlin Drive, San Diego, CA 92121-4794
www.advantagebooksonline.com

ISBN 1-57145-472-1
Library of Congress Cataloging-in-Publication Data
available upon request.

1 2 3 4 5   00 01 02 03 04

Publisher: **Penny Martin**
Consultants: **Geoff Bryant and Geoffrey Burnie**
Managing editor: **Jane Warren**
Text and picture research: **Susan Page and Karen Winfield**
Design: **Juno Creative Services, Sydney; Bob Mitchell**
Cover design: **James Mills-Hicks**
Page makeup: **Arc Typography, Sydney**
Production manager: **Linda Watchorn**
Film separation: **Pica Colour Separation, Singapore**
Printed by: **Dah Hua Printing Co. Ltd, Hong Kong**

CONTENTS

INTRODUCTION

ANNUALS are a group of plants which complete their whole life cycle—germination through to full maturity, setting seed and decline—within one growing season, or one year. Biennials, by contrast, complete their life cycles over two seasons often merely establishing their foliage in the first season and waiting for the subsequent season to flower. Perennials live at least three seasons, but some, which will grow from seed or cuttings and will flower in their first year— such as petunias and impatiens— are treated as annuals.

Under artificial conditions, annuals can be encouraged to germinate and flower early, with the result that garden suppliers and nurseries have year-round stocks of instant color, in the form of mature annuals either on the point of flowering, or in full bloom. For gardeners in colder parts of the world, the sight of a pot of vibrant pansies in early spring can chase away the gloom of the last grey days of winter.

Use in the garden

Annuals are the answer for the impatient gardener of the new Millennium; perhaps the closest we can get to instant color and immediate gratification in the garden.

The accelerated life span of annuals is perfect for the gardener who requires a floral show, either for a particular event, such as a garden wedding, or merely as a visual foil for the green shrubs and trees which make up the framework of most gardens. They are useful also in the new garden, providing visual interest—in the color of flowers, texture of the foliage or form of

A tub of Viola x wittrockiana *'Jolly Joker' is guaranteed to dissolve winter blues*

Cascading petunias and pelargoniums soften this semi-formal garden

the plant—while the slower-growing perennials and shrubs become established, or while the final design for the garden is still under discussion.

Annuals are suitable for planting in all types of containers, such as window boxes or pots, and when planted like this, they have the added advantage of being movable, so that they can be used to brighten up a dull area of the garden, or liven up the view from a window. Trailing annuals, such as the Pendula petunias and lobelia, are particularly popular for the hanging basket displays which soften and beautify many a courtyard setting. In Britain, where hanging baskets have become almost an art form, it is now possible to have them planted up for you by garden centers and nurseries, using the plants of your choice, and even the irrigation, until now perhaps the greatest challenge with hanging baskets, is taken care of by hidden reticulation sprinklers.

We are all familiar with the sight of extravagant beds of flowering annuals in public parks and large corporate gardens; yet gardens of any size—or even the smallest roof garden, balcony or windowsill—can play host to the colors and fragrances offered by this diverse group of plants. And of course, many annuals are perfectly happy indoors, on a windowsill or in the con-servatory, where the colors and scent of the flowers can be enjoyed at close range.

Growing habits and effects

Annuals represent a wide variety of growing habits, from creeping, ground-hugging plants like portulaca, through tall larkspur, trailing petunias and the bushy forms of marigold, to the twining climbers, such as the vibrant nasturtium.

While annuals are generally associated with colorful floral display, in fact many are worth growing for their foliage alone; coleus and bloodleaf, both perennials which are treated as annuals, are good examples. Fragrant annuals such as evening primrose are candidates for courtyard containers and bed borders near to the house, where their fragrance is most likely to be noticed, and are ideal for the edges of paths, where a brush by a passer-by will release the scent.

The heady fragrance and myriad colors of Lathyrus odoratus *'Special Mixed' make a winning cut flower combination*

Annuals which make good cut flowers include the cornflower, sweet pea (*Lathyrus odoratus*), *Clarkia* and the long-lasting *Eustoma grandiflorum*, while the attractive seed heads of some, such as the poppy and *Nigella*, are popular for dried floral arrangements.

Starting out...and getting results

Annuals are easy to grow from seed, given the appropriate care and conditions. You can raise seedlings yourself, or, if you prefer, you can buy trays of seedlings from garden centers. They are a very versatile group of plants which are relatively inexpensive, widely available, resilient and adaptable, though when you choose your plants, it is worth remembering that they are native to temperate and subtropical climates.

The local climatic conditions will determine when, or if, annual seeds should be planted outdoors. When there is any risk of a late frost, it is generally safest to germinate the seeds of frost tender annuals in a greenhouse, or indoors, on a warm, closed verandah or in a windowsill propagator, and then plant out the sturdy seedlings when spring is well under way. These annuals tend to flower in summer and autumn. The seeds of frost hardy annuals, such as pansies and the Iceland poppy, can be sown in the autumn and left to over-winter, ready to flower in spring.

Choose the position of your annuals carefully, since the art of a successful garden lies in putting plants in the right place. With this in mind, plant annuals in outside beds where the plants will get the benefit of lots of sunlight, especially morning sun, and remember to make the beds wide enough to prevent the annuals from being overwhelmed by shrubs and perennials which will fill up the beds as the season progresses. Try planting annuals with perennials so that as one group fades, another can take center stage, and your garden will never lack color or variety.

Prepare the beds by weeding, then digging over the topsoil to the depth of a fork, removing to one side, and then digging the lower layer to the same depth. This is known as double digging. Fork in some compost or well-rotted manure before replacing the topsoil—this step is essential, since annuals need a rich soil medium if they are to perform well. If the seeds of frost hardy annuals are to be sown directly

Paved paths create a sense of order in this garden, while annuals and perennials provide height and color

into the soil, as in temperate climates, it is important at this stage to rake over the soil surface, breaking up any large clods.

When planting out seedlings, make holes a suitable distance apart using a dibble or pencil; separate the roots of seedlings carefully and ensure that the seedlings stay at the same soil level as in the seed tray. Firm down the soil around each seedling and water.

Feeding and watering annuals correctly depends on the species, but there are some general considerations too. Annuals achieve a huge amount of growth in a short season, making them very demanding of their soil medium, and planting them in a compost-rich, fertile soil, with added fertilizer, makes more sense than trying to supplement the nutrition of a plant established in a poor soil. Nevertheless, powdered or liquid fertilizer can be used to help maintain growth of healthy plants. If you use the same annuals bed year after year, remember to add a good measure of compost every year, some weeks before you plant your seedlings.

Use drip lines or perforated soak hoses, rather than overhead sprinklers, to water annuals, but avoid over-watering, as this encourages fungal disease.

Deadhead regularly to encourage new heads, and to keep the plants tidy. However, it is worth bearing in mind that annuals are temporary plants, and should be treated as such, so once they are past their best, discard them and prepare the soil for fresh plantings.

Pests and diseases will vary depending on the plant type and the climatic conditions, so if the condition of a plant deteriorates, ask your local garden center or nursery for advice. In general, a plant which is coping with adverse growing conditions will be more susceptible to disease than one which is growing under ideal conditions. Seedlings, however, are always vulnerable to attack by chewing pests and birds, although only slugs and snails are likely to do any significant harm. Drench seedlings regularly in a fungicidal solution to ward off the fungal disease damping off, which causes them to collapse.

Annuals and perennials in containers and unstructured beds lend a relaxed atmosphere to a spring garden

ABELMOSCHUS

The some 15 species in this genus used to be classified as part of the genus *Hibiscus*. Natives of tropical Africa and Asia, they are hairy annuals, biennials or short-lived perennials with tough bark and maple-like leaves. Most species are grown for their flowers, although the bark of some is used as fiber, and *Abelmoschus esculentus* is a tropical crop, grown for its edible seed pods (okra and gumbo). Some species die back to a large tuber in the dry season. The flowers are hibiscus-like and may be shades of yellow, pink, orange or red.

CULTIVATION Mostly grown as summer annuals, they need fertile, well-drained soil, a sheltered site in full sun, and lots of water. Propagate from seed in spring. Rust disease can be a problem: spray with a fungicide.

Abelmoschus moschatus
Musk mallow

This musk-scented, Asian species is variable, with many wild and cultivated forms. The (musk) seeds yield oils and fats (ambrette) used medicinally and in perfumery; some forms are valued for fiber. The hairs on the leaves are often bristly and the large flowers are typically pale yellow with a purple eye. Ornamental cultivars come in a range of colors. The compact **'Mischief'** grows well in pots or can be naturalized in a sunny, sheltered site; red, pink or white flowers

Abelmoschus m. 'Pacific Orange Scarlet'

are borne in summer and fall (autumn). Dwarf **'Pacific Light Pink'** is only 18 in (45 cm) tall with 2-tone pink flowers up to 4 in (10 cm) wide. **'Pacific Orange Scarlet'** (syn. 'Oriental Red') is very popular.

ZONES 8–12.

AGERATUM

Floss flower

While many gardeners will be familiar with the annual bedding plants that are derived from *Ageratum houstonianum*, this genus in fact includes some 43 species of annuals and perennials, mostly native to warmer regions of the Americas. These mound- and clump-forming plants grow to a height of 30 in (75 cm), and are characterized by hairy, oval to heart-shaped leaves which have subtly serrated edges. The flower-heads, crowded in terminal clusters, are a mass of fine filaments, usually dusky blue, lavender or pink.

CULTIVATION They prefer full sun and moist, well-drained soil. Deadhead the faded flowers regularly, to prolong the flowering season. In spring, propagate from seed either sown in indoor containers or directly outdoors (in milder climates).

Ageratum houstonianum

Ageratum houstonianum

This clump-forming annual, native to Central America and the West Indies, is valued as a summer bedding plant; its foliage and dusky blue, fluffy flowers blend well with many other bedding plants. Pink and white forms also exist. Tall, medium and dwarf sizes reach 12 in (30 cm), 8 in (20 cm) and 6 in (15 cm) in height, respectively.

ZONES 8–12.

AGROSTEMMA

This genus is related to *Lychnis* and *Silene* and comprises 2 or more species of slender annuals from the

Mediterranean region. Although one of them is regarded in Europe as a crop weed, it is an appealing plant with large rose-pink flowers and is therefore sometimes grown in meadow plantings and cottage gardens. The leaves have long, silky hairs and the distinctive calyx has 5 very long, leaf-like sepals which radiate well beyond the petals.

CULTIVATION These plants are very frost hardy; they thrive in full sun in a well-drained soil. Space young plants to about 10 in (25 cm) apart. In exposed areas, plants may need staking. Propagate from seed sown in early spring or fall (autumn).

Agrostemma githago
Corn cockle

A fast growing, showy annual which grows as high as 24–36 in (60–90 cm), making it ideal as the backdrop for shorter plants in a border. It is slender and willowy, with few branches, and has long, narrow leaves in opposite pairs. The pink flowers are shaped like an open broad trumpet and are about 2 in (5 cm) across; they appear on long hairy stalks from late spring to early fall (autumn). The tiny dark brown seeds are poisonous.

ZONES 8–10.

Agrostemma githago

ALCEA
Hollyhock

Linnaeus used both the old Roman name, *Alcea*, and the name *Althaea* (from the Greek *altheo* 'to cure') to describe this genus which was used in traditional remedies. The common name hollyhock derives from 'holy hock' or 'holy mallow', and it is said that plants were taken to England from the Holy Land during the Crusades from their native eastern Mediterranean. There are about 60 species in the genus, all from western and central Asia. They produce flower spikes which may be 6 ft (1.8 m) or more high, making them far too tall for the average flowerbed; even 'dwarf' cultivars grow to 3 ft (1 m) tall.

CULTIVATION Although they are fairly frost hardy, they need protection from wind, and they should be staked if grown in an exposed site. They prefer sun, a

Alcea rosea

rich, heavy well-drained soil and frequent watering in dry weather. Propagate from seed in late summer or spring. Rust disease can be a problem; spray with fungicide.

Alcea rosea

syn. *Althaea rosea*
Hollyhock

This erect biennial is believed to originate from Turkey or Palestine and is grown for its tall flower spikes which appear in summer and early fall (autumn), and come in colors including pink, purple, cream and yellow. Flowers can be either single, flat circles of color 4 in (10 cm) across, or so lavishly double that they are like spheres of ruffled petals. Leaves tend to

be rounded and rough. Plants are usually unbranched and grow up to 10 ft (3 m). Cultivars include **Chater's Double Group** (peony-shaped, double flowers in myriad colors), **Pinafore Mixed** and **Majorette Mixed** (lacy, semi-double flowers in pastel shades).

ZONES 4–10.

AMARANTHUS

This is a genus which includes weeds, leaf vegetables, grain crops and ornamentals grown for their brilliant foliage, curious flowers and adaptability to hot, dry conditions. It comprises some 60 species of erect, spreading or prostrate annuals and short-lived perennials, distributed through most warmer parts of the world. They are popular bedding plants, with large, attractively colored leaves and minute flowers borne in pendent, catkin-like spikes.

CULTIVATION They are marginally frost hardy and in cool climates are usually brought on under glass before planting out in late spring. A sunny, dry position with shelter from strong winds is essential, and they grow well in fertile, well-drained soil. Prepare soil for planting with plenty of manure and water seedlings regularly. Mulch during hot weather. Prune the young plant to thicken growth. Watch for snails, caterpillars and aphids. Propagate from seed.

Amaranthus caudatus
Love-lies-bleeding, tassel flower

This is a fascinating plant with dull green leaves and dark red flowers in long, drooping cords, their ends often touching the ground. It grows to 4 ft (1.2 m) or more high. Flowers appear in summer through to fall (autumn). Traditionally, this plant was used to give height to the center of circular beds.

ZONES 8–11.

AMMI

Half a dozen or more annuals and biennials belong to this genus, occurring wild in the Mediterranean region, western Asia and the Canary Islands. They feature large, ferny basal leaves and flowering stems bearing large umbels of numerous small white flowers. *Ammi* was the classical Greek and Latin name for a plant of this type, though its exact identity is uncertain. *Ammi visnaga* has long been used medicinally in the Middle East and *A. majus* is used as a cut flower.

CULTIVATION They are easy to grow in a sheltered, sunny position

Amaranthus caudatus

Ammi majus

in any reasonable garden soil, kept fairly moist. Propagate from seed in spring. They will usually self-seed once established.

Ammi majus
Bishop's weed

Originally from the Mediterranean and western Asia, this species has become widely naturalized in other continents. A succession of large, lacy flowering heads appear in summer and fall (autumn). They are sometimes sold as cut flowers. Plants grow to about 24–36 in (60–90 cm) tall.

ZONES 6–10.

Useful Tip

Overwinter young pimpernel plants in a greenhouse until the danger of frost has passed.

ANAGALLIS
Pimpernel

A genus of about 20 species of low-growing annuals and perennials with small, elliptical to heart-shaped, bright green leaves arranged in opposite pairs. A profusion of small, 5-petalled flowers appear in spring and summer; the solitary, bell- or open saucer-shaped flowers often arise from the leaf axils or occasionally in small racemes at the stem tips. Flowers come in colors including pink, orange, red, blue and white.

CULTIVATION Plant in full sun in any well-drained soil that does not dry out entirely in summer. The more attractive, less vigorous species are excellent rockery plants. Propagate annuals from seed; perennials from seed, by division or from small tip cuttings. Some of the weedy species self-sow readily.

Anagallis monellii
syns *Anagallis linifolia*, *A. collina*

The tiny, brilliant blue or scarlet flowers of this summer-flowering little plant are only ½ in (12 mm) in diameter. This species grows no taller than 18 in (45 cm), with a spread of at least 6 in (15 cm).

ZONES 7–10.

Anagallis monelli

ANCHUSA

Alkanet, summer forget-me-not

Many of the plants in this genus have a weedy growth habit, but they are worth growing for their striking blue flowers, which last well and attract bees. Flowering occurs from spring through to summer. About 50 species of annuals, biennials and perennials make up the genus, occurring in Europe, North and South Africa and western Asia. They are ideal for beds, borders and containers; the dwarf perennials are best in a rock garden.

CULTIVATION Frost hardy, they grow best in a sunny position in deep, rich, well-drained soil. In very hot areas, some shade will help maintain the flower color. Feed sparingly, water generously and stake taller plants. The root systems can be extensive, so give them plenty of room. Cut back spent flower stalks after flowering to promote new growth. Propagate annuals and biennials from seed in fall (autumn) or spring, perennials by division in winter. Transplant perennials when dormant in winter.

Anchusa capensis
Cape forget-me-not

In cool climates, this southern African species is biennial, but in warm-temperate climates it can be sown in early spring to bear intense blue flowers in summer. It grows to 15 in (40 cm) tall and wide. Grown as an annual, '**Blue Angel**' achieves a height and spread of 8 in (20 cm), with shallow, bowl-shaped, sky blue flowers in early summer. '**Blue Bird**' is 24 in (60 cm) tall and equally striking.

ZONES 8–10.

Anchusa capensis

Anchusa capensis 'Blue Angel'

ANTIRRHINUM

Snapdragon

The Ancient Greek name for the snapdragon flower was 'Antir-rhinon', meaning 'nose-like'. In French they are known as 'gueule de loup' (meaning 'wolf's mouth'), and in German and Italian their name means 'lion's mouth'. Most of the some 40 species of these annuals, perennials and evergreen subshrubs originate in the western Mediterranean region, a few from western North America.

CULTIVATION They prefer fertile, well-drained soil in full sun. Propagate *Antirrhimun majus* from seed in spring or early fall (autumn).

Antirrhinum majus

Garden snapdragon

This perennial, valued for its showy flowers borne over a long period from spring to fall (autumn), should be treated as an

Antirrhinum majus

annual—it rarely flowers well after the first year, and old plants are susceptible to the fungus, antirrhinum rust. The many cultivars, mainly grown as annuals, spread 12–18 in (30–45 cm) and may be tall, 30 in (75 cm); medium, 18 in (45 cm); or dwarf, 10 in (25 cm). Deadhead to prolong flowering and pinch out early buds to increase branching. New hybrids are bred for their tolerance to bad weather, height, large blooms, colors and uniformity.

ZONES 6–10.

ARCTOTIS

syns *Venidium* x
Venidioarctotis
African daisy

This genus consists of about 50 species of annuals and evergreen perennials from dry stony sites in South Africa. The stems and leaves are coated in matted downy hairs, giving them a gray-green or silver-gray color. The flowers, which are typical of the daisy family, are reliant on the sun to open fully; they come in creamy yellow through orange to deep pinks and claret reds. Many hybrids exist, their blooms characterized by dark rings near the center. Plants may be compact and shrubby to quite prostrate, the lower-growing types forming a fast growing and colorful ground cover.

CULTIVATION They do well if given plenty of space in full sun and well-drained, sandy soil. Deadhead after the first flush of early summer flowers fade to prolong flowering. Propagate from seed or cuttings, which can be rooted at any time of year.

Arctotis Hybrids

Known until recently as x *Venidioarctotis* hybrids, one of the main parent species having being placed in the genus *Venidium* (now combined with *Arctotis*), they are grown as annual bedding plants in frost-prone areas but will overwinter in milder climates. They grow to a height and spread

Useful Tip

When cutting snapdragons for flower arrangements, or when tidying spent stalks, cut the stalks back to 2-3 in (5-7 cm) from the crown, to promote new blooms on long stalks.

of around 18 in (45 cm). The gray, lobed leaves are quite downy on their undersides. In summer and fall (autumn) they produce a long succession of showy blooms, up to 3 in (8 cm) across, in a very wide range of colors, often 2-toned. **'Gold Bi-Color'**, **'Apricot'**, **'Flame'**, **'Dream Coat'** and **'Wine'** are the more popular hybrids.

ZONES 9–11.

Arctotis Hybrid 'Flame'

Useful Tip

Arctotises may be used to rapidly cover a large area of bare, dry bank.

Arctotis Hybrid 'Apricot'

Arctotis Hybrid 'Dream Coat'

B

BEGONIA

Begonia

There are over 1500 known species of begonias, distributed in moist tropical and subtropical regions of all continents except Australia; the most diverse are found in South America. Mostly evergreen, they vary from low-growing rhizomatous perennials to 10 ft (3 m) shrubs. Many are valued for their foliage, which may be beautifully textured and colored, or for their flowers, or indeed both. The broad, often asymmetrical leaves are slightly brittle with a waxy texture. Female flowers, as distinct from male flowers on the same plant, have broad, colored flanges on the ovaries, which develop into winged fruits.

Begonias are classified according to growth habit and type of rootstock: **cane-stemmed** begonias are erect, sometimes quite tall, with straight stems, fibrous roots and often pendent clusters of showy flowers; **shrubby** begonias are similar, with a more closely branched habit (the bedding begonias belong here); **winter-flowering** begonias have lower, softer stems and profuse, colorful flowers; **rhizomatous** begonias, a large and varied class (the **Rex** begonias with colorful, variegated leaves and others

Begonia, Semperflorens-cultorum Group

grown for foliage belong here), have leaves arising from rhizomes; and the **tuberous** begonias, (including the **Tuberhybrida Group**), which bear large, showy, often double flowers in summer, and die back to tubers in winter.

CULTIVATION Many cane-stemmed, winter-flowering, shrubby and rhizomatous types can be grown outdoors in frost-free climates. Grow potted plants indoors in good light with good ventilation and above-average humidity. Pinch back young, shrubby begonias to keep them compact and to encourage flowers. The tubers of tuberous begonias must be forced into growth in early spring at a temperature of 65°F (18°C) in peat moss or sphagnum, and kept in a cool, well-ventilated greenhouse for summer flowering. Lift the tubers in mid-fall (mid-autumn) and store dry. Propagate tuberous begonias from tubers; other types from stem or leaf cuttings, by division of rhizomes, or from seed. Gray mold (botrytis) and powdery mildew can be a problem if conditions are too warm and damp. Slugs and snails are especially fond of rhizomatous begonias.

Begonia, **Semperflorenscultorum Group**
Bedding begonia, wax begonia

These dwarf, shrubby begonias, derived mainly from the Brazilian *Begonia semperflorens*, are often grown as bedding annuals (for example '**Ernst Benary**'), for borders in shaded gardens, or in containers. Freely branching with soft, succulent stems, their rounded, glossy green (bronze or variegated in some cultivars) leaves are about 2 in (5 cm) long. They flower profusely over a long summer and early fall (autumn) season, or most of the year in warmer climates. Numerous cultivars exist: singles and doubles in bright rose pink, light pink, white or red, often released as a series with mixed colors. Propagate from seed or stem cuttings planted out in late spring in cooler climates. Pinch back growing tips to encourage bushy growth. Most popular are the bushy miniatures of the **Cocktail Series** ('**Gin**', '**Vodka**' and '**Whiskey**') and the compact mixed pink and white '**Thousand Wonders**'.

ZONES 9–11.

Useful Tip

To propagate non-tuberous begonias from leaf cuttings, lay the cut leaf blades on damp sand and weigh them down with pebbles.

BELLIS

Daisy

Bellis is from the Latin *bellus*, meaning 'pretty' or 'charming', while the common name is a corruption of 'day's eye', a reference to the way the flowers close at night, and open to greet the sunrise. These, the true daisies, are some 15 species of small perennials that occur wild in Europe, North Africa and Turkey. Small oval to spoon-shaped leaves form rosettes, each rosette producing a succession of flowerheads on individual stalks in shades of white, pink, blue or crimson. Only one of the species is widely grown, mostly in the form of improved strains.

CULTIVATION They thrive in any good garden soil in sun or part-shade; keep soil moist in winter and spring. They are popular as spring-flowering edging plants, and though perennial in cool-temperate climates, they are usually treated as annuals or biennials. Propagate from seed in fall (autumn) or by division.

Bellis perennis
English daisy, common daisy

This daisy has become widely naturalized in temperate parts of most continents. Wild plants are small, forming carpets of crowded rosettes that spread through lawns by short runners. The flowerheads, 1 in (25 mm) wide, are white with golden centers and pale purple undersides, and appear from late winter to early summer. The garden strains mostly have double flowerheads of red, crimson, pink or white, all with a gold center. Cultivars include: **'Medicis White'** (white) and **'Alba Plena'** (double white). The **Pomponette Series** daisies have neat, hemispherical flowerheads 1½ in (35 mm) wide with curled petals, on stems up to 10 in (25 cm) high, in mixed colors; they are popular as bedding plants and cut flowers.

ZONES 3–10.

Bellis perennis in lawn

BORAGO

This genus comprises 3 species of annuals and short-lived perennials, all of which are native to rocky sites in western, central and eastern Europe. They generally exhibit an erect, somewhat coarse growth habit. The stems are hairy, as are the simple, alternate lance-shaped leaves. In spring, clumps of basal leaves rapidly develop into branched, leafy flowering stems, and by late spring, the plants bear nodding, starry purple-blue or white flowers. The flowers are attractive and, as a rich source of nectar, are popular with beekeepers.

CULTIVATION They are easy to grow in any light, moist, well-drained soil in full sun. In general, they are propagated from seed sown *in situ* in spring; the annual species can be sown in late winter for an early crop. They tend to self-seed readily, which means that they may become slightly invasive. Protect from snails.

Borago officinalis
Borage

This robust, annual herb is grown for its cucumber-flavored, lance-shaped leaves and its pretty, purplish blue star-shaped flowers. The plant grows to around 30 in (75 cm) in height and bears branched cymes of 5-petalled flowers over a long period in spring and summer. The fresh young leaves are used in cold drinks, eaten raw in salads and are cooked with vegetables. The flowers too are edible and are popular for decorating salads.

ZONES 5-10.

Borago officinalis

BRACHYCOME

syn. *Brachyscome*

Botanists disagree over the spelling of this genus: named *Brachyscome* (*brachys* 'short' and *kome* 'hair') by a nineteenth-century botanist, he later corrected his poor Greek and dropped the middle 's'. The low-growing annuals and evergreen perennials of this Australian genus make ideal ground cover or rockery plants. Many of the perennials form mounds, spreading by underground runners and having finely divided, soft, fern-like foliage. They bear a profusion of daisy-like flowerheads in shades of blue, mauve, pink and yellow, with orange or brownish centers (or yellow as in the hybrids **'Sunburst'** and **'Outback Sunburst'**, both with white ray florets).

CULTIVATION Many are moderately frost hardy and some will tolerate coastal salt spray. They need a sunny aspect and prefer a light, well-drained garden soil and dry conditions. Pinch out early shoots to encourage branching and propagate from ripe seed or stem cuttings or by division in spring or fall (autumn).

Brachycome iberidifolia 'Blue Star'

Brachycome iberidifolia

Brachycome iberidifolia
Swan River daisy

This weak-stemmed annual, grown as a bedding or border plant, grows to a height and spread of around 12 in (30 cm), sometimes taller. Its leaves are deeply dissected and have very narrow segments. A profusion of small, fragrant, daisy-like flowerheads appear in summer and early fall (autumn); normally mauve-blue they are sometimes white, pink or purple. **'Blue Star'** has massed mauve to purple-blue flowers.

ZONES 9–11.

BRACTEANTHA
syn. *Helichrysum*
Strawflower, everlasting daisy

Until recently part of *Helichrysum*, this Australian genus of 7 species of annuals and perennials is now distinct. They differ from true helichrysums in their large, decorative flowerheads carried singly or a few together at the end of the flowering branches, each consisting of golden yellow to white papery bracts surrounding a disc of tiny yellow or brownish florets. The mostly broad, thin leaves are often

Bracteantha bracteata

downy beneath and can be very sticky in some species. Most of the cultivated forms and seedling strains are treated as forms of *Bracteantha bracteata*, but further botanical study is likely to result in new species being recognized.

CULTIVATION They do well in moist, well-drained soil in full sun. The summer-flowering annuals may be planted from late winter for an early display. Most species will tolerate light to moderate frosts as long as they don't get too wet. Propagate annuals from seed and perennials from seed or tip cuttings.

Bracteantha bracteata
syn. *Helichrysum bracteatum*

An erect annual or short-lived perennial which grows to about 3 ft (1m), this species has weak, hollow stems and thin green leaves. From summer to early fall (autumn) it bears golden-yellow blooms up to 2 in (5 cm) across. **Bright Bikinis Series** is a modern descendant of vigorous annuals

developed in the mid-nineteenth century, with larger flowerheads in shades of pink, bronze red, cream, purple and yellow. Some more spreading, shrubby perennial plants from eastern Australia, which may be recognized as distinct species, have been named as cultivars: **'Dargan Hill Monarch'** and **'Diamond Head'** are two examples.

B R O W A L L I A

Bush violet, amethyst violet

Native to tropical South America and the West Indies, the 6 species of bushy annuals and evergreen perennials in this genus have dense foliage and a compact habit. Their stems are soft and their leaves simple, strongly veined and deep green. The flowers are similar to the related nicotianas, but are smaller and have shorter tubes. Carried singly in the leaf axils, the flowers may be profuse on healthy plants. Shades of blue, purple or white are most common.

CULTIVATION In cool climates, grow them as conservatory plants or as summer annuals. In frost-free climates, they will do well outdoors in moist, humus-rich, well-

---

Useful Tip

Bracteantha bracteata *is a good cut flower, and may be dried for winter decoration too.*

drained soil in a warm, part-shaded position sheltered from drying winds. Feed regularly with liquid fertilizer to keep foliage lush and to promote flowering. Pinch back stem tips to encourage bushiness. Propagate annuals from seed in spring, perennials from seed or tip cuttings.

Browallia americana
syn. *Browallia elata*

This bushy annual, up to 24 in (60 cm) tall, bears showy flowers in summer and early fall (autumn). The flowers are 2 in (5 cm) wide and colors vary from a rare intense blue through paler violet to white. This versatile plant grows well outdoors and is also a good pot plant. **'Vanja'** has deep blue flowers with white eyes; **'White Bells'** has ice white flowers.

ZONES 9–11.

Browallia americana

C

CALCEOLARIA

Ladies' purse, slipper flower, pocketbook flower

Many people are familiar with the brilliant slipper flowers sold by florists. In fact, there are more than 300 species in this genus, ranging from tiny annuals to herbaceous perennials and even scrambling climbers and quite woody shrubs, all native to the Americas, from Mexico south to Tierra del Fuego. The flowers of all species share the curious feature of a bulbous lower lip, the so-called 'slipper'. Flowers are mainly yellows and oranges, often with red or purple spots.

CULTIVATION Calceolarias come from a wide range of natural habitats and vary greatly in their tolerance to cold. They prefer a shady, cool site in moist, well-drained soil with added compost. Protect the delicate flowers from wind. Prune back shrubby species by half in winter. Propagate from seed or softwood cuttings in summer or late spring.

Calceolaria, Herbeohybrida Group

These hybrids—the florists' calceolarias—are bushy, soft-stemmed and compact biennials often treated as annuals and are derived from 3 Chilean species. They bloom in spring and summer in colors from yellow to deep red and so densely massed they almost hide the soft green foliage. Innumerable named varieties have appeared over the years, now mostly sold as mixed-color seedling strains and series.

Calceolaria, Herbeohybrida Group

Calceolaria, Herbeohybrida Group, 'Sunset Mixed'

They can be used for summer bedding but are intolerant of very hot, dry conditions and only marginally frost hardy. Normally 12-18 in (30–45 cm) tall, dwarf strains can be as small as 6 in (15 cm). **'Sunset Mixed'** and **'Sunshine'** are two F1 hybrids popular for massed bedding.

ZONES 9–11.

CALENDULA

Marigold

St Hildegard of Bingen (1098–1179) is believed to have dedicated *Calendula officinalis* to the Virgin Mary, giving rise to the name 'Mary's gold', or 'marigold'. In the Middle Ages, marigolds were used as a remedy for 'evil humors of the head', indigestion and even smallpox and even today, marigold is a favorite in herbal remedies. The so-called 'African' and 'French' marigolds are *Tagetes* from Mexico and are unrelated to *Calendula*, which comprises 20-odd species of bushy annuals and evergreen perennials native to the Canary Islands, across the Mediterranean region to Iran. Their simple leaves are aromatic and the daisy-like flowers are orange or yellow.

CULTIVATION Mostly fairly frost-hardy, these plants are easy to grow in well-drained soil of any

Calendula officinalis

quality, in sun or part-shade. Regular deadheading prolongs flowering. Propagate from seed, and watch for aphids and powdery mildew.

Calendula officinalis

Pot marigold, English marigold

Originally native to southern Europe and long valued for its medicinal qualities, only the cultivars and seedling strains are grown in gardens. These winter- and spring-flowering, bushy annuals have a long flowering season. All have lance-shaped, aromatic, pale green leaves and single or double flowerheads. Tall forms reach a height and spread of 24 in (60 cm) and include **'Geisha Girl'** (double orange flowers); the **Pacific Beauty Series** (double flowers in many colors including bicolors); **'Princess'** (crested orange, gold or yellow flowers); and the **Touch of Red Series** (double, deep orange-red flowers). Dwarf cultivars, only 12 in (30 cm) tall, include **'Fiesta Gitana'** (double flowers in cream to orange) and **'Honey Babe'** (apricot, yellow and orange flowers).

ZONES 6–10.

CALLISTEPHUS

China aster

The sole species in this genus is an annual, native to China and once included in the genus *Aster*. A colorful summer-flowering plant, it is popular both for bedding and as a cut flower, since it comes in an array of colors from white to pink, blue, red and purple. There are many variants and strains are added almost annually. The 3-4 in (8–10 cm) flowerheads can be either yellow-centered single daisies or fully double; doubles' petals may be plume-like and shaggy, more formal and straight or very short, making a pompon-like shape.

CULTIVATION Although usually sown in spring for summer flowering, it is best to make successive sowings to prolong the flowering season. It will grow in any climate, from the coolest temperate to subtropical, and it will thrive in sunshine and fertile, well-drained soil. This is a superb cut flower.

Callistephus chinensis
syn. *Aster chinensis*

This is an erect, bushy, fast growing annual with oval, toothed, mid-green leaves and long-stalked

Callistephus chinensis

flowerheads. Many seedling strains are available, ranging from tall, up to 3 ft (1 m), to dwarf, about 8 in (20 cm) tall. Stake tall plants and deadhead. The **Milady Series** are vigorous growers, up to 12 in (30 cm) in height, with double flowers in pink, red, white, purplish blue or mixed colors.

ZONES 6–10.

Useful Tip

Do not plant Callistephus *in the same bed 2 years in a row—a rest of 2 or 3 years between plantings is desirable to guard against aster wilt, a soil-borne fungus.*

CAMPANULA

Bellflower, bluebell

Most of the some 250 species of showy herbaceous plants in this genus are perennials, but there are a few annuals and biennials. All are native to the temperate parts of the northern hemisphere. The variable leaves mainly arise from upright stems or are sometimes only in basal clusters. Flowers tend to be bell-shaped, but may be tubular, cup-or star-shaped, mainly in blues and purples with some pinks and whites. Campanulas are useful for rockeries, borders, wild gardens and hanging baskets.

CULTIVATION They vary from very frost hardy to frost tender. All thrive in moderately rich, moist, well-drained soil, in sun or shade, but flower color is best in shady sites. Protect from drying winds and stake the taller plants which make good cut flowers. Cut back spent flower stems. Propagate from seed in spring—sow alpines in fall (autumn)—by division in spring or fall (autumn), or from basal cuttings in spring. Transplant during winter and watch for slugs.

Campanula medium
Canterbury bell

A slow growing, erect biennial with narrow basal leaves, it comes from southern Europe. In spring and early summer it forms 4 ft (1.2 m) spires of crowded, white, pink or blue, bell-shaped flowers with recurved rims and prominent large green calyces. Dwarf cultivars grow to 24 in (60 cm), and the colored calyx of double forms is like a second petal tube. Grow as border plants in part-shade.

ZONES 6–10.

Campanula medium

CATHARANTHUS

Madagascar periwinkle

Sometimes wrongly referred to as *Vinca*, this quite distinct genus comprises 8 species of annuals and evergreen perennials or subshrubs, all originally from Madagascar. *Catharanthus roseus* has spread throughout warmer regions of the world and is the only species widely grown as bedding and border plants and sold as potted plants. The stems are repeatedly branched and fleshy and the leaves are plain and smooth edged. The flowers are clustered in the upper leaf axils and resemble oleanders, with a short tube opening by a very narrow mouth into 5 flat, radiating petals.

CULTIVATION Grow in a sunny conservatory or as a summer bedding plant in cooler areas. In warm climates they are moderately tolerant of deep shade, strong sun and a dry atmosphere. Grow in free-draining soil kept moist in the growing period. Prune the tips to promote bushiness, but not so heavily as to inhibit flowering. Propagate from seed or from cuttings in summer.

Catharanthus roseus cultivar

Catharanthus roseus

syns *Lochnera rosea, Vinca rosea*
Pink periwinkle

The wild form of this shrubby perennial is about 24 in (60 cm) high, with white to rose pink flowers deepening to a darker red center. Garden forms are lower, more compact and have larger flowers in a wider range of colors. They flower mainly in spring and summer in cooler climates, almost year-round in warm climates. The flowers of some mixed-color series range from purple through pink to white; others have pale colors (or white) with prominent red eyes. All plant parts contain poisonous alkaloids from which drugs of value in the treatment of leukaemia have been refined.

ZONES 9–12.

Catharanthus roseus cultivar

Useful Tip

Get into the habit of weeding little and often; that way you remove the weeds before they set seed and you cut down on future weeding.

CELOSIA

Cockscomb, Chinese woolflower

More than 50 species of erect annuals, perennials and shrubs make up this genus of the amaranthus family from warmer parts of the Americas, Asia and Africa; only *Celosia argentea* is widely cultivated as a bedding annual and for cut flowers. Numerous forms have evolved; while all have simple, soft and strongly veined leaves, the structure of the small flowerheads varies markedly between the 2 main cultivated races.

CULTIVATION In cooler climates, grow in a conservatory or plant out as summer bedding after raising seedlings under glass in spring. Better suited to warmer climates, they are tolerant of the fiercest heat. Plant in full sun in rich, well-drained soil and water freely in dry weather. Propagate from seed in spring.

Celosea argentea, Cristata Group

Celosia argentea

syns *Celosia cristata,*
C. pyramidalis

An erect, summer-flowering annual which reaches at least 3 ft (1 m), it is probably native to tropical Asia. The leaves are mid-green; the silvery white flowers appear on spikes with a silvery sheen. It is best known for two very different cultivar groups: the **Plumosa Group**, with plumes of tiny deformed flowers in a range of hot colors, and the **Cristata Group** (cockscombs), with wavy crests of fused flower stalks in many colors. Seedling strains of both differ in height as well as size and the color of the flowers. The Plumosa Group is especially popular as cut flowers and indoor pot plants. Some dwarf strains are no more than 6 in (15 cm) tall, while the old-fashioned bedding strains are about 24 in (60 cm) tall. Most strains are sold as mixed colors.

ZONES 10–12.

Celosia argentea, Plumosa Group, Century Series

CENTAUREA

Cornflower, knapweed

This genus is part of the thistle tribe of composites and has around 450 species of annuals, biennials and perennials distributed all over the temperate, grassy regions of Eurasia and north Africa, with one or two in America. Some are regarded as weeds in some parts of the world. The blue cornflower *Centaurea cyanus* is a well-known garden annual and some of the perennials are valued; they come in various colors, from white through shades of blue, red, pink, purple and yelow.

Flowerheads have a characteristic urn-shaped receptacle of fringed or spiny bracts, from the mouth of which radiate the quite large florets, each deeply divided into 5 colored petals; they lack a distinct central disc, as compared with other members of the daisy family.

CULTIVATION They thrive in well-drained soil in a sunny site. Propagate from seed in spring or fall (autumn); perennials can also be divided in spring or autumn.

Centaurea cyanus

Centaurea cyanus

Blue-bottle, bachelor's button, cornflower

This annual is not only a common weed of cereal crops, but also a well-loved wildflower of Europe and northern Asia. It grows about 24-36 in (60–90 cm) tall, has weak stems, very narrow leaves and small, shaggy flowerheads that are typically a slightly purplish shade of blue. Garden varieties have been developed with larger flowers in shades of pale and deep pink, cerise, crimson, white, purple and blue, some of them dwarf and more compact. Most striking if planted in a large clump, it will flower for months if regularly deadheaded.

ZONES 5–10.

'Chrysanthemum' carinatum

'CHRYSANTHEMUM'

The once large and varied genus of *Chrysanthemum* has been the subject of much confusion for many years. Once it contained not only the florists' chrysanthemums but several other related groups such as the shasta daisies, marguerites, tansies and pyrethrums. For a while, florists' chrysanthemums were given their own genus, *Dendranthema*, but a recent decision by an international committee on botanical nomenclature has brought their scientific name back into line with popular usage and they have now had the name *Chrysanthemum* restored to them. The painted daisy, along with the corn marigold and crown daisy is now considered to belong to a separate genus from the florists' chrysanthemums. They are likely to become the new Dendranthemas (in a direct swap with florists' chrysanthemums), but meanwhile their genus name remains *'Chrysanthemum'*, in quotes.

CULTIVATION The 3 *'Chrysanthemum'* annuals are easily grown in any good garden soil in a sunny site. They prefer coolish summers but can be timed in warmer, drier climates to bloom in winter. Sow seed in spring in cool climates or in fall (autumn) in warmer climates.

'Chrysanthemum' carinatum

syn. *'Chrysanthemum' tricolor*
Painted daisy, summer chrysanthemum, tricolor chrysanthemum

This Moroccan plant grows to 24 in (60 cm), spreading to about 12 in (30 cm) wide and is excellent as a cut flower or bedding plant. It has much-divided, rather fleshy leaves and bears banded, multicolored flowers in spring and early summer. **'Monarch Court Jesters'** is either red with yellow centers or white with red centers; the **Tricolor Series** has many color combinations.

ZONES 8–10.

CLARKIA

syn. *Godetia*

This genus of bushy annuals, allied to *Oenothera*, was named after Captain William Clark, of the famous Lewis and Clark expedition that crossed the American continent in 1806. It consists of about 36 species, and has unre-

Clarkia amoena cultivars

markable foliage but spectacular funnel-shaped flowers in various shades of pink, white and carmine. The showy flowers, which resemble azaleas (in Germany their name means 'summer azalea'), can be 4 in (10 cm) across. They are very good as cut flowers, borne on long stems and lasting a week in water.

CULTIVATION Easy to grow in full sun in any temperate climate, they prefer moist but well-drained, slightly acid soil; soil that is too fertile will see good foliage but poor flower production. Propagate from seed in fall (autumn) or spring.

Clarkia amoena
syn. *Clarkia grandiflora*
Farewell-to-spring

This native of California is a free flowering, fast growing annual, reaching a height of 24 in (60 cm) and spread of 12 in (30 cm). Its leaves are lance shaped and mid-green and it has thin, upright stems. In summer, spikes of open, cup-like, single or double flowers in shades of pink appear. There are a number of cultivars. Allow it to dry out between watering and watch for signs of botrytis.

ZONES 7–11.

Useful Tip

Create a windbreak and you will have less need to stake tall plants, and there will be less damage after storms.

CLEOME

Spider flower, spider plant

Some 150 species of bushy annuals and short-lived evergreen shrubs, distributed in mountain valleys and plains in subtropical and tropical zones worldwide, make up the genus. Flowers are characteristically spidery, with 4 petals that narrow into basal stalks and mostly long, spidery stamens and styles. The leaves are composed of 5-7 palmate leaflets. One species, widely grown as a background bedding plant, is valued for its rapid growth and delicate flowers.

CULTIVATION Marginally frost hardy, they require full sun and fertile, well-drained soil, regular water and shelter from strong

Cleome hassleriana

winds. Remove side branches to promote taller growth and dead-head regularly. Propagate from seed in spring or early summer. Check for aphids.

Cleome hassleriana
syn. *Cleome spinosa* of gardens

This native of subtropical South America has distinctive, spidery flowers. A fast growing, erect plant, it reaches 4 ft (1.2 m) tall with a spread of 18 in (45 cm). It has large palmate leaves and hairy, slightly prickly stems which in summer are topped with heads of fragrant pink and white flowers with long, protruding stamens. Several cultivars, available as seed, range from pure white to purple.

ZONES 9–11.

CONSOLIDA
Larkspur

The name *Consolida* dates back to Medieval times, when it was given in recognition of the plants' use in the healing of wounds: they were believed to help with blood clotting (consolidating). The common name refers to the nectar spur at the back of the flowers, clearly visible on the unopened buds. Although these annuals, about 40 species in all, were once treated as part of the

Delphinium genus, they are now considered distinct. They occur wild in the Mediterranean region and as far as west and central Asia. Garden larkspurs are mostly derived from *Consolida ajacis* and include many strains, mostly grown as mixed colors. They have finely divided, feather-like leaves, poisonous seeds and spurred, delphinium-like flowers in pink, white or blue. The flowers of the taller types last well as cut flowers.

CULTIVATION They will succeed in any temperate or even mildly subtropical climate; they prefer full sun and rich, well-drained soil. Stake tall cultivars. Propagate from seed sown direct in clumps about 8-12 in (20-30 cm) apart. Watch for snails and slugs and for powdery mildew.

Consolida ajacis
syns *Consolida ambigua*, *Delphinium consolida*

This Mediterranean species originally had blue flowers. Modern garden larkspurs, known as 'rocket

larkspurs', are the result of crossing this species with *Consolida orientalis*; the 'forking larkspurs' may be derived mainly from *C. regalis*. The mainly summer flowers may be pink, white or purple and are usually double. Some can be as tall as 4 ft (1.2 m).
ZONES 7–11.

Consolida ajacis

CONVOLVULUS

This genus includes slender, twining creepers and small herbaceous plants from many temperate regions of the world. Only a few are shrubby, and even these are soft-stemmed and renewed by shooting from the base. The leaves are simple and often narrow and the flowers form a strongly flared tube that opens by unfurling 'pleats'. In contrast with morning glories (*Ipomoea*), which shrivel by mid-morning or early afternoon, *Convolvulus* flowers stay open all day. Flowers usually bloom over a long season.

CULTIVATION They will grow in most soils and in either sheltered or exposed sites, but they prefer full sun. Prune hard after flowering to thicken growth. Sow seed of annuals *in situ* in mid-spring, or in fall (autumn), protected from frost with cloches. Propagate perennials from cuttings.

Convolvulus tricolor 'Blue Ensign'

Convolvulus tricolor
syn. *Convolvulus minor*

A mass of deep purple-blue or white flowers with banded yellow and white throats characterizes this bedding annual from the Mediterranean. A slender, few-branched plant, it grows to a height of 8-12 in (20–30 cm) and has small, lanceolate, mid-green leaves. Flowering is from late spring to early fall (autumn), each flower lasting only one day. **'Blue Ensign'** has very deep blue flowers with pale yellow centers.

ZONES 8–11.

COREOPSIS

Some 80 species of annuals and perennials make up this genus of the daisy family which is native to cooler or drier regions of the Americas. In summer, flowerheads borne on slender stems appear; they are mostly shades of gold or yellow, but may be bicolored. Leaves vary from simple, narrow and toothed, to deeply divided and may be basal or scattered up the stems. The annuals are grown as summer bedding plants, whereas the perennials are grown in borders.

CULTIVATION Annuals prefer full sun and a fertile, well-drained soil; they will not tolerate heavy clay soil. Perennials prefer full sun and a fertile, well-drained soil but also grow well in coastal regions and in poor, stony soil. Propagate by dividing old clumps in winter or spring, or by spring cuttings. Stake tall varieties. Propagate from seed in spring or fall (autumn).

Coreopsis tinctoria

Useful Tip

The best mulches are organic materials (such as straw, leaf litter or bark chips) which allow rainwater and air to reach the topsoil; they also feed and improve soil texture as they break down.

Coreopsis tinctoria

Tickseed, plains coreopsis, calliopsis

Clusters of bright yellow flowerheads with red centers appear on this fast growing, showy annual during summer and fall (autumn). It grows 24-36 in (60–90 cm) tall, but it tends to lean over and may need staking. It provides good cut flowers.

ZONES 4–10.

COSMOS

Mexican aster

The 25 annuals and perennials in this genus are allied to *Dahlia*; one or two are well-known garden plants. They have erect but weak, leafy stems and the leaves are either lobed or deeply and finely dissected. The daisy-like flowerheads are borne on slender stalks that terminate branches and feature showy, broad ray-florets surrounding a small disc; they range from white through pinks, yellows, oranges, reds and purples to deep maroon.

CULTIVATION In cold climates they need protection as they are only moderately frost hardy. Plant out seedlings only once all danger of frost has passed. They like a sunny aspect with protection from strong winds and will grow in any well-drained soil as long as it is not over-rich. Mulch with compost and water well in hot, dry weather. Propagate annuals from seed in spring or fall (autumn), perennials from basal cuttings in spring. Deadhead regularly, and in humid weather check for insect pests and mildew.

Cosmos bipinnatus

Common cosmos, Mexican aster

This is a feathery-leafed annual from Mexico and far southern USA which grows 5-6 ft (1.5–1.8 m) tall. It bears daisy-like flowerheads in summer and fall (autumn), in shades of pink, red, purple or white. Taller plants may need staking. Newer strains are usually more compact and may have striped or double flowers. 'Sea Shells' has usually pink, sometimes crimson or white flowerheads with edges of ray-florets curled into a tube.

ZONES 8–11.

Cosmos bipinnatus

CYNOGLOSSUM

Thus genus, which consists of 55 species of annuals, biennials and perennials from most temperate regions of the world, is valued for its long flowering period. The flowers resemble the common forget-me-not, to which they are related.

CULTIVATION All the species are frost hardy and require a fertile but not over-rich soil; if over-nourished the plants tend to flop over. Propagate from seed sown in fall (autumn) or spring or, in the case of perennial species, by division.

Cynoglossum amabile

Cynoglossum amabile
Chinese forget-me-not

This upright annual or biennial reaches a height of about 20 in (50 cm). It has dull green, hairy, lanceolate leaves and bears flowers in racemes—generally blue although white and pink forms can occur. Flowers are produced in spring and early summer. It self-seeds very readily. **'Firmament'** has pendulous sky blue flowers.

ZONES 5–9.

Cynoglossum amabile 'Firmament'

DELPHINIUM

Some 250 or so species belong in this genus, including self-seeding annuals, dwarf alpine plants and tall perennials that can exceed 8 ft (2.4 m). They are distributed in the temperate zones, mainly of the northern hemisphere, with a few found at high altitude in Africa. Nearly all form a tuft of basal leaves on long stalks, their blades divided into 3 to 7 radiating lobes or segments. The tufts elongate into erect, sometimes branched flowering stems that bear stalked, 5-petalled flowers, each with a nectar spur at the back. Named groups include the Belladonna, Elatum and Pacific hybrids.

CULTIVATION Most like a cool to cold winter and are very frost hardy. Grow in full sun with well-drained, fertile soil with plenty of organic matter. Protect from high winds and stake tall plants. Feed with liquid fertilizer every 2–3 weeks. Propagate from seed (annuals and biennials) or cuttings or by division (perennials). Some species have been bred true from seed.

Delphinium, Pacific Hybrids

These hybrids, though short-lived perennials, are usually grown as annuals or biennials. They derive mainly from *Delphinium elatum*, and were bred in California. They grow as tall as 5 ft (1.5 m) or more,

Delphinium, Pacific Hybrid, 'Black Knight'

and bear clusters of star-like single, semi-double or double flowers, mainly blue, purple or white, on erect spikes. Cultivars range from white ('**Galahad**') through sky blue ('**Summer Skies**') and pale purple ('**Guinevere**') to lavender ('**Astolat**') and purple with white eyes ('**King Arthur**') or black eyes ('**Black Knight**').

ZONES 7–9.

Delphinium, Pacific Hybrid, 'Galahad'

Useful Tip

Delphiniums will respond well to feeding with liquid fertilizer every 2-3 weeks.

DIANTHUS

Carnation, pink

Of the some 300 species in the genus, one species comes from Arctic North America, a few from southern Africa, and the vast majority occur in Europe and Asia. The name 'pink' refers to the ragged edge of the petals, which look as if they have been cut with pinking shears. Hybrids have been bred for particular purposes: Border Carnations, used in borders and for cut flowers; Perpetual-flowering Carnations and American Spray Carnations, often grown under cover for cut flowers; perfumed Malmaison Carnations, named after the Bourbon rose '**Souvenir de la Malmaison**' which they resemble; Modern Pinks and Old-fashioned Pinks bred for cutting and the garden; and Alpine or Rock Pinks, used mostly in rock gardens. In all groups, some cultivars are self-colored while others are flecked, picotee or laced; the latter 2 types having petal margins of a different color. Most are rock garden or edging plants.

CULTIVATION Varying from fully to marginally frost hardy, they like a sunny site, protection from strong winds, and well-drained, slightly alkaline soil. Stake taller varieties. Prune stems after flowering. Propagate annuals and biennials from seed in fall (autumn) or early spring; perennials by layering or from cuttings in summer. Watch for aphids, thrips and caterpillars, rust and virus infections.

Dianthus barbatus
Sweet William

Sweet William is often treated as a biennial, though it is a short-lived perennial which self-sows readily and is ideal for massed planting. It is frost hardy and grows 18 in (45 cm) high and 6 in (15 cm) wide. The fragrant flowers are borne in flattened heads and may be white through pinks to carmine and crimson-purple; they are often zoned in two tones. They appear in late spring and early summer. Dwarf cultivars, about 4 in (10 cm) tall, are usually treated as annuals. 'Sweet Wivelsfield' is a hybrid strain from a cross with Modern Pinks.

ZONES 4–10.

Dianthus chinensis
Chinese pink, Indian pink

This annual from China is low-growing, tufted, and has gray-green, lance-shaped leaves. In late

Dianthus barbatus

Dianthus chinensis 'Strawberry Parfait'

spring and summer it bears masses of single or double, sweetly scented flowers in shades of pink, red, lavender and white. It is slow growing to a height and spread of 6–12 in (15–30 cm), and is fully frost hardy. **'Strawberry Parfait'** has fringed, single pink flowers with deep red centers.

ZONES 7–10.

DIMORPHOTHECA

African daisy, Cape marigold

This South African genus, related to *Osteospermum*, comprises 7 species of annuals, perennials and evergreen subshrubs known for their colorful, daisy-like flowers

which appear from late winter. The flowers close on cloudy days. They are well suited to rock gardens and borders, containers and bedding.

CULTIVATION Moderately hardy, they like an open, sunny aspect and fertile, well-drained soil; they are salt tolerant. Deadhead to prolong flowering and prune lightly after flowering. Propagate annuals from seed in spring and perennials from cuttings in summer. Watch for fungal diseases in climates with summer rainfall.

Useful Tip

Weed the garden regularly and use traps or barriers to deter snails.

Dimorphotheca pluvialis
syn. *Dimorphotheca annua*
Rain daisy

The small but striking flowers are pure white above, purple beneath with brownish purple centers and are borne in late winter and spring. This low-growing annual reaches 8-12 in (20–30 cm) tall and wide.

ZONES 8–10.

Dimorphotheca pluvialis

DOROTHEANTHUS

Ice plant,
Livingstone daisy

This South African genus consists of about 10 species of succulent, mat-forming annuals. Summer-flowering, they bear a profusion of dark-centered, gaudy red, pink, white or bicolored daisy-like flowers. They are ideal for borders and massed displays.

CULTIVATION Marginally frost hardy, they grow in well-drained soil in a sunny position. Deadhead to prolong flowering and keep tidy. In frost-prone areas plant out once the danger of frost has passed. Propagate from seed.

Dorotheanthus bellidiformis

Useful Tip

The Livingstone daisy is perfect for carpeting a dry slope with low-fertility soil with magnificent results!

Dorotheanthus bellidiformis

Ice plant, Livingstone daisy, Bokbaai vygie

This small succulent annual grows to 6 in (15 cm) in height and spreads to 12 in (30 cm). Its daisy-like flowerheads in dazzling shades of yellow, white, red or pink open in summer sun, but close in dull weather. It has fleshy, light green leaves up to 3 in (7 cm) long with glistening surface cells.

ZONES 9–11.

ERYSIMUM

syn. *Cheiranthus*
Wallflower

This genus now includes *Cheiranthus* and consists of 80 species of annuals and perennials from Europe to central Asia, a few from North America. Some are suitable for rock gardens; others do well in a border. Short-lived species are best grown as biennials. Some are winter- to spring-flowering plants, while others, grown in mild climates, will bloom all winter or all year round. Older types have a sweet fragrance; newer cultivars, although unscented, have a longer flowering period.

CULTIVATION Mostly frost hardy, they do best in well-

Erysimum cheiri 'Monarch Fair Lady'

drained, fertile soil in an open, sunny site. Trim perennials after flowering to keep the plant tidy. Propagate from seed in spring or cuttings in summer.

Erysimum cheiri
syn. *Cheiranthus cheiri*
English wallflower

This bushy species from southern Europe has been grown in cottage gardens for centuries, and is grown as an annual or biennial. Cultivars vary in height from 8-24 in (20–60 cm) and spread to 15 in (38 cm); all have lanceolate leaves. In spring (or mild winters), fragrant 4-petalled flowers appear in colors from pastel pink and yellow to deep brown, bronze, orange, bright yellow, dark red and scarlet. They do best where summers are cool. '**Monarch Fair Lady**' grows to 18 in (45 cm) high and has single, deep orange to bright yellow flowers; '**Orange Bedder**' grows to 12 in (30 cm) high and has scented, brilliant orange flowers.

ZONES 7–10.

Useful Tip

One way to maintain high humidity for your indoor pot plants is to stand the pot on a tray of pebbles and water.

Erysimum cheiri

ESCHSCHOLZIA
California poppy

The poet and botanist Adalbert von Chamisso (1781–1838) named this genus from western North America after his friend Johan Friedrich Eschscholz. It comprises 8-10 sun-loving annuals and perennials which feature deeply dissected leaves, capsular fruits and bright yellow to orange poppy-like flowers that close up in dull weather.

CULTIVATION They thrive in warm, dry climates in poor, well-drained soil but are also tolerant of quite severe frosts. They resent being disturbed, so sow the seed directly where they are to grow. Deadhead regularly to prolong flowering. Propagate from seed in spring.

Eschscholzia californica

Eschscholzia californica

The vivid orange, cup-shaped flower of this species is the official floral emblem of California. The foliage is feathery and gray-green; of rounded habit, it grows to about 12 in (30 cm) high and wide. It flowers in spring with intermittent blooms in summer and fall (autumn) but the flowers close at night and on dull days. Named cultivated strains may have bronze, yellow, cream, scarlet, mauve and rose blooms and include '**Mission Bells Mixed**', '**Ballerina**' and the compact '**Thai Silk Series**'.

ZONES 6–11.

Useful Tip

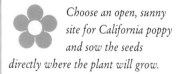

Choose an open, sunny site for California poppy and sow the seeds directly where the plant will grow.

E U P H O R B I A

Milkweed, spurge

Close to 2000 species belong in this genus, among them annuals, biennials, perennials, subshrubs, trees, and numerous succulent species which bear a remarkable resemblance to cacti. Most are tropical and subtropical, though there are many temperate species. Despite the great variety of forms, the flowers of all species are almost identical: very much reduced, consisting of only a stigma and a stamen, always green, and usually carried in small clusters. Species with showy bracts are the most widely grown.

CULTIVATION Thriving in sun or part-shade in moist, well-drained soil, they vary from frost hardy to tender, depending on the species; the succulent species tend to be frost tender. Propagate from seed in fall (autumn) or spring, from cuttings in spring or summer (allowing succulent species to dry and callus before placing in barely damp sand), or by division in early spring or fall (autumn).

Euphorbia marginata
Snow on the mountain, ghostweed

This attractive, bushy annual makes an unusual cut flower, and is a good foil for brighter flowers in the garden or vase. Native to central areas of North America, it has pointed, oval, bright green leaves sharply margined with white, and broad, petal-like white bracts surrounding small flowers in summer. It grows fairly rapidly to about 24 in (60 cm) tall and about 12 in (30 cm) wide. It is tolerant of cold.

ZONES 4–10.

EUSTOMA

syn. *Lisianthius*

This genus of 3 species of annuals, biennials and perennials, ranging in the wild from southern USA to northern South America, is a member of the gentian family. *Eustoma grandiflorum* in particular is popular as a cut flower and has been the subject of considerable breeding work. The color range now includes the original violet, as well as white, pale blue and pink; double flowers are available too.

CULTIVATION Easy to grow in any warm-temperate climate, they need only sun, perfect drainage and fertile soil. They are frost tender and rarely do well after the first year. Propagate from seed in spring or from cuttings in late spring or summer.

Euphorbia marginata

Eustoma grandiflorum cultivar

Eustoma grandiflorum
syn. *Lisianthus russellianus*
Prairie gentian, Texas bluebell,
lisianthus

This erect biennial, native to the American Midwest, provides superb cut flowers which last up to 3 weeks in water; it is also suitable as a container plant. It has gray-green leaves and 2 in (5 cm) wide, flared, tulip-like flowers in rich purple, pink, blue or white. It grows slowly to a height of 24 in (60 cm) and spread of 12 in (30 cm).

ZONES 9–11.

EXACUM

Like *Eustoma* a member of the gentian family, this genus comprises about 25 species of annuals, biennials or perennials, widely distributed through tropical Africa and Asia. The flat or broadly cup-shaped flowers are mainly yellow, white, blue or purple. Only *Exacum affine* is widely grown.

Useful Tip

A cut flower arrangement of Eustoma grandiflorum *will give you weeks of pleasure; even the unopened buds on the spray will open in the water.*

Exacum affine

CULTIVATION They need a warm, frost-free climate and they do best in a sunny site in rich, moist but well-drained soil. Grown indoors, they prefer filtered sun and temperatures above 50°F (10°C). Propagate from seed in early spring.

Exacum affine
Persian violet, German violet

This miniature plant from the hot, dry island of Socotra, just off the horn of Africa at the mouth of the Red Sea, is grown as an indoor plant, popular for its neat, shrub-like habit and long succession of flowers. Small, 5-petalled, saucer-shaped, usually purple-blue flowers with yellow stamens appear all through summer. A biennial usually treated as an annual, it achieves a height and spread of 8-12 in (20–30 cm). Dwarf cultivars '**Blue Midget'** (lavender-blue flowers) and '**White Midget'** (white flowers) are half as big.

ZONES 10–12.

GHI

GAILLARDIA

Blanket flower

The blanket flower is so-called because the vivid colors of its daisy-like flowers (reds, yellows and oranges) echo those of blankets traditionally worn by Native Americans. They are a colorful asset to a flower border and meadow garden, and are also good cut flowers. This genus of around 30 species of annuals, perennials and biennials are all native to the USA, with the exception of 2 South American species. The perennials are better suited to cool-temperate climates. The flowering season is very long: from summer until the first frosts. The flowers are either single, like small sunflowers, or double and as much as 6 in (15 cm) wide.

CULTIVATION They are very hardy and tolerate extremes of heat, cold and dryness as well as strong wind and poor soil. They prefer full sun in well-drained soil. Stake taller plants. In cool climates, cut the stems of perennials back in late summer. Propagate from seed in spring or early summer, or divide perennials in spring.

Gaillardia pulchella

This frost-hardy upright annual or, rarely, short-lived perennial, rapidly reaches 18–24 in (45–60 cm) in height and 12 in (30 cm) in spread. It has hairy, lanceolate, gray-green leaves. The summer flowers have red ray florets with yellow tips or self-colored red or yellow with a cone-shaped

Gaillardia pulchella 'Lorenziana'

purplish disc-floret. Deadhead regularly to prolong the already long flowering season.

ZONES 8–10.

GYPSOPHILA

Some of the some 100 species of annuals and perennials in this genus from Europe, Asia and North Africa are semi-evergreen. The narrow leaves are borne in opposite pairs. *Gypsophila* is grown for its abundant, dainty white or pink flowers which are very popular with florists.

CULTIVATION   Fully   frost hardy, they will tolerate most soils, but do best in deep, well-drained soil lightened with compost or peat, and thrive in limy soil. Most dislike wet winter conditions. Choose a site in full sun, and protect the plant from strong winds. Cut back after flowering to encourage   a   second   flush. Transplant when dormant during winter. Propagate from seed in spring or fall (autumn) or from cuttings in summer.

Gypsophila paniculata
Baby's breath

This short-lived perennial is usually grown as an annual. It reaches a height and spread of 3 ft (1 m) or

Gypsophila paniculata

more. It has small, dark green leaves and sprays of tiny, white spring flowers. **'Bristol Fairy'** has double white flowers. **'Compact Plena'** has double white or soft pink flowers.

ZONES 4–10.

HELIANTHUS

All of the some 70 species of annuals and perennials in this genus of the daisy family are native to the Americas. The genus includes plants used for livestock fodder, the Jerusalem artichoke, an important oilseed plant and many ornamentals. The leaves are hairy, often sticky and the stems are tall and rough. Large, daisy-like, usually golden-yellow flowerheads are on prolonged display from summer to fall (autumn).

Helianthus annuus

CULTIVATION They are frost hardy, prefer full sun and like a well-drained soil. They need shelter from high winds. Fertilize in spring to promote large blooms and water generously in dry conditions. Cut perennials back to the base after flowering. Propagate from seed or by division in fall (autumn) or early spring.

Helianthus annuus 'Teddy Bear'

Helianthus annuus
Common sunflower

This well-known giant annual grows rapidly to a height of 10 ft (3 m) or more, and in summer bears large, daisy-like, 12 in (30 cm) wide, yellow flowerheads with brown centers. The leaves are broad and mid-green. This species produces one of the world's most important oilseeds. It can be a little large for small gardens, but varieties of a more manageable size—about 6 ft (1.8 m)—include **'Autumn Beauty'** and the double-flowered **'Teddy Bear'**.

ZONES 4–11.

HIBISCUS

Best known for the countless culti- vars of *Hibiscus rosa-sinensis*, this diverse genus of around 220 species includes annuals and perennials, as well as hot-climate evergreen shrubs, small trees and deciduous, temperate-zone shrubs. The leaves are mostly toothed or lobed and the flowers, borne singly or in ter- minal spikes from spring to fall (autumn), are characteristic: fun- nel-shaped, with 5 overlapping petals and a central column of fused stamens.

CULTIVATION Generally easy to grow, the shrubby species do best in full sun and slightly acid, well-drained soil. Water regularly and feed during the flowering peri- od. Trim into shape after flower- ing. Propagate from seed or cut- tings or by division, depending on the species. Check for aphids, mealybugs and white fly.

Hibiscus trionum
Bladder ketmia,
flower-of-an-hour

This fast growing species, found in warm regions worldwide, may be an annual or biennial herb or subshrub, growing 3 ft (1 m) high and 24 in (60 cm) wide. The leaves are hairy, palmately divided and toothed. A scattering of small, pale yellow flowers with a deep crimson, almost black center appear each morning in summer and fall (autumn). It self seeds readily.

ZONES 9–11.

Hibiscus trionum

IBERIS

These annuals, perennials and evergreen subshrubs are mainly from southern Europe, northern Africa and western Asia. The 50 species of this genus are valued for their flowers and are decorative in borders, bedding and rock gardens. The showy flowers are borne either in erect racemes of pure white, or as flattish heads in white, red and purple.

CULTIVATION Fully to marginally frost hardy, they require a warm, sunny position and a well-drained, light soil, preferably with added lime or dolomite. Propagate from seed in spring or fall (autumn) or cuttings in summer. They may self-seed, but are unlikely to become invasive.

Iberis amara
Candytuft, hyacinth-flowered candytuft

The purplish white or white scented flowers of this frost-hardy, fast growing and erect bushy annual are borne in domed racemes in early spring and summer. It has lance-shaped, mid-green leaves and reaches a height of 12 in (30 cm), with a spread of 6 in (15 cm). Various strains are available. The large, fragrant, pink flowers of the **Hyacinth-flowered Series** are good cut flowers.

ZONES 7–11.

Iberis amara cultivar

IMPATIENS

Most gardeners know the value of *Impatiens* in summer bedding and container planting; the name is a reference to their vigor. This genus of around 850 species of succulent-stemmed annuals, evergreen perennials and subshrubs is widely distributed, especially in the subtropics and tropics of Asia and Africa. The range of flower colors is always increasing. In colder climates, many of the mild-climate perennial hybrids are grown as annuals.

CULTIVATION Varying from frost hardy to frost tender, they will grow in sun or part-shade; many do well under overhanging trees. They prefer a moist, free-draining soil, and need shelter from strong winds. Tip prune the fast growing shoots to promote bushiness and flowering. Propagate from seed or stem cuttings in spring and summer.

Impatiens balsamina
Garden balsam

This erect, bushy annual from India, China and Malaysia grows fairly quickly to a height of 12–18 in (30–45 cm) with a spread of 8–10 in (20–25 cm). It has lance-

Useful Tip

When growing Impatiens *from seed, press the seeds lightly into the top of the seed-raising mix and don't cover them: they need light for germination.*

shaped bright green leaves and small, camellia-like single or double spurred flowers throughout summer and early fall (autumn). Colors include blood red, purple-red, pink and white; some may be spotted. It is marginally frost hardy and is ideal for bedding in full sun.

ZONES 9–12.

Impatiens balsamina

Impatiens walleriana
syn. *Impatiens sultanii*
Busy Lizzie

Originally from tropical East Africa, this succulent, evergreen perennial is grown as a summer-flowering annual in frost-prone regions. In shady, frost-free gardens, it makes a bushy plant with masses of flowers almost year-round. Its stems are soft and fleshy with reddish stripes, the leaves are oval and a crisp green and the flat, spurred flowers are crimson, ruby red, pink, orange, lavender or white, even variegated. It is marginally frost hardy and fast growing, reaching a height and spread of 12–24 in (30–60 cm). There are many cultivars.

ZONES 9–12.

Impatiens walleriana

Impatiens walleriana

IRESINE

This group of 80 evergreen tropical species from the Americas and Australia—annuals, climbing perennials and subshrubs of the amaranthus family—are grown for their striking, colorful foliage, which provides an interesting contrast to flowering plants. They vary in habit from upright to ground hugging. The white or green flowers are insignificant.

CULTIVATION They are frost tender and only make permanent garden plants in frost-free, warm climates. In cooler areas they can be grown in greenhouses and planted out once all chance of frost has passed. They do well in loamy, well-drained soil and must be kept moist during the growth period. Grow in full sun for best leaf color. Pinch the growing tips to promote bushiness. Propagate from cuttings in spring.

Useful Tip

The color in your garden need not be confined to the flowers: coleus and Iresine herbstii *will brighten up garden beds without so much as a flower between them.*

Iresine herbstii
syn. *Iresine reticulata*
Beefsteak plant, bloodleaf

This annual or short-lived perennial species from Brazil makes an attractive bedding or pot plant. While it can achieve a height of 24 in (60 cm) and a spread of 18 in (45 cm), plants grown as annuals are much shorter. In cold climates, it should be overwintered as struck cuttings in a greenhouse. The stems are red and the leaves—rounded, purple-red with notches at the tips and yellowish red veins—are up to 4 in (10 cm) long. Garden forms range from bright green leaves with bright yellow veins, through to rich purple-green leaves and beetroot-pink veins (**'Brilliantissima'**).

ZONES 10–12.

Iresine herbstii 'Brilliantissima'

L

LATHYRUS

This genus of 150 or so species of annuals and perennials, some of them edible, are allied to both the garden pea *(Pisum)* and vetch *(Vicia)*. They are native mainly to temperate northern hemisphere regions, but with a significant number also in Andean South America. They are grown for their showy pea-like, often scented flowers which come in a wide range of colors, from red, mauve and white to blue and even pale yellow. The leaves are pinnate, the uppermost pair of leaflets often forming tendrils which allow the plant to climb. Flat seed pods follow the flowers. *Lathyrus odoratus* was one of the main plants used by Gregor Mendel (1822–84) in his studies on genetics.

CULTIVATION These frost-hardy plants like fertile, well-drained soil in full sun. Stake or train on wires and deadhead regularly. Propagate annuals from seed in early summer or early fall

Lathyrus odoratus 'Katherine'

(autumn); perennials from seed in fall (autumn) or by division in spring. Mildew and botrytis may affect them.

Lathyrus odoratus
Sweet pea

The cultivated form is a great improvement on the wild form from Italy: it is a vigorous climbing annual, grown for its abundant, fragrant flowers of white, cream, pink, blue, mauve, lavender, maroon and scarlet. Flowers appear, several to a stem, from late winter to early summer and make excellent cut flowers. The plant grows to 6 ft (1.8 m) or more in height; dwarf, non-climbing cultivars also exist. Climbers need good support, such as wire netting or trellis, and are useful for covering sunny walls or fences. With breeding, flowers have become less fragrant, and mixed-color strains (like 'Carnival') tended to predominate, but a new range of fragrant, self-colored cultivars has emerged: 'Apricot Sprite', 'Bandaid', 'Elegance', 'Esther Ranson', 'Felicity Kendall', 'Hampton Court', 'Katherine', 'Kiri Te Kanawa' and 'Lucy'. The **Knee-hi Group**, around 24 –30 in (60–75 cm) high, is a bushy strain, as is the **Supersnoop Group**, which lack tendrils.

ZONES 4–10.

Useful Tip

Train sweet peas along a North-South oriented wall or trellis to catch the maximum amount of sun.

Lathyrus odoratus 'Carnival'

Lathyrus odoratus Supersnoop Group cultivar

LAVATERA

The 25 species of annuals, biennials, perennials and softwooded shrubs in this genus have a scattered distribution around temperate regions of the world, mostly in Mediterranean or similar climates, and often grow in dry, rocky, even coastal places. Closely related to the mallows and hollyhocks, a few are grown for their colorful mallow flowers which bloom over a long season. These plants are upright in habit with simple to palmately lobed leaves, often downy to the touch. The annuals, biennials and short-lived perennials are suitable for summer bedding or border planting.

CULTIVATION Moderately to very frost-hardy, these plants prefer a sunny site in any well-drained soil. Prune after flowering to encourage branching and more blooms. Propagate annuals, biennials and perennials in spring or early fall (autumn) from seed sown *in situ*, and shrubs from cuttings in early spring or summer.

Lavatera trimestris
Annual mallow

This Mediterranean shrubby annual is grown for its silken, trumpet-shaped, brilliant white or pink flowers. The flowers, which are 3 in (8 cm) wide, appear from summer to early fall (autumn); they are short lived but abundant

Lavatera trimestris

Lavatera trimestris 'Silver Cup'

and benefit from deadheading. It has an erect, branching habit and grows reasonably rapidly to a height of 24 in (60 cm) and a spread of 18 in (45 cm). Cultivars include the white **'Mont Blanc'** syn. *Lavatera* 'Mont Blanc' and deep pink **'Silver Cup'**.

ZONES 8–11.

Lavatera trimestris 'Mont Blanc'

LEUCANTHEMUM

This genus from Europe and temperate Asia comprises about 25 species of annuals or perennials and was previously included in *Chrysanthemum*. The leaves are toothed or lobed and long-stalked, daisy-like flowerheads arise from leafy stems. Flowers have yellow disc florets and white or yellow ray florets. Although generally undemanding, some species may be reluctant to grow in warmer climates.

CULTIVATION These plants grow well in full sun or morning shade in moderately fertile, moist but well-drained soil. Propagate from seed, cuttings or by division.

Leucanthemum paludosum 'Show Star'

Leucanthemum paludosum
syn. *Chrysanthemum paludosum*

This southern European annual grows to 6 in (15 cm) in height. It has pale yellow or white-tinged yellow flowers. **'Show Star'** has bright yellow flowers and wavy-margined leaves.

ZONES 7–11.

LIMNANTHES
Meadow foam

The 7 species in this genus are wild meadow plants of western North American; only *Limnanthes douglasii* is widely grown, and mainly elsewhere. The 5-petalled, cup-shaped flowers and bright green leaves provide reliable color from spring to fall (autumn).

CULTIVATION They thrive in damp soil and full sun, but must have cool roots. Sow seed directly in fall (autumn) or early spring and

Limnanthes douglasii

lightly cover. Stagger sowing to ensure a prolonged floral display. They suit a rockery or path edge.

Limnanthes douglasii
Meadow foam, poached egg flower

This delicate, colorful plant grows only 6 in (15 cm) high. It has pale green, ferny foliage and masses of 1 in (25 mm), slightly perfumed, white-edged flowers with golden central 'yolks'; a plain gold form also exists. The species name is given in honor of the early nineteenth-century collector David Douglas, who made many important finds in western North America.

ZONES 8–10.

Limonium sinuatum, Petite Bouquet Series

Useful Tip

Limnanthes douglasii *is highly attractive to bees, as are hollyhocks,* Anchusa, Phacelia *and* Reseda *species*

LIMONIUM
Statice, sea lavender

These plants are often grown in the gardens of seaside holiday homes because they are tolerant of sea spray and low rainfall and are generally undemanding. The some 150 species in this genus are scattered around the world's temperate regions, often in saline coastal and desert environments, with major concentrations in the Mediterranean, central Asia and the Canary Islands. They include evergreen and deciduous subshrubs, annuals, biennials and perennials. The tapered, almost stalkless leaves form basal rosettes. The many-colored, papery flowers of some annual species make good cut and dried flowers.

CULTIVATION Statices are easily grown in full sun and well-drained, sandy soil and they do well in coastal gardens. Lightly fertilize plants in spring, while the flowerheads are developing. Propagate from seed in early spring or fall (autumn), by division in spring, or from root cuttings in late winter. Transplant during winter or early spring.

Limonium sinuatum
syn. *Statice sinuata*

This bushy Mediterranean perennial is a popular cut flower and almost invariably grown as an annual. It grows dense rosettes of oblong, wavy-margined leaves and a profusion of tiny, papery flowers on winged stems. It flowers in summer and early fall (autumn) and is fairly slow growing, reaching a height of 18 in (45 cm) and a spread of 12 in (30 cm). Seedling strains are available in a range of colors. Dwarf plants in the **Petite Bouquet Series**, only 12 in (30 cm) tall, have golden- or lemon-yellow, white, cream, salmon-pink, purple or blue spikelets.

ZONES 9–10.

LINARIA
Eggs and bacon, toadflax

These 100 species of annuals, biennials and perennials mainly from the Mediterranean region and western Europe have naturalized widely. They are valued for their masses of tiny snapdragon-like flowers in a range of colors. Their erect stems grow to 18 in (45 cm)

Limonium sinuatum

with stalkless, usually gray-green leaves. *Linaria* is an ideal candidate for a cottage garden, rock garden or border.

CULTIVATION They require rich, well-drained, preferably sandy soil, moderate water and full sun. Seed sown directly in fall (autumn) or very early spring will germinate in 2 weeks. Cut back after flowering to ensure a second flush.

Linaria maroccana
Baby snapdragon, toadflax

Native to Morocco but naturalized in northeastern USA, this annual is a useful bedding plant, its small blooms giving a prolonged spring display in gold, pink, mauve, apricot, cream, purple and yellow. Fast growing and bushy, it has lance-shaped, pale green leaves and grows to a height of 4–6 in (10–15 cm) and spread of 4 in (10 cm). **Fairy Bouquet** is a mixed-color strain.

ZONES 6–10.

Useful Tip

Keep Linaria *seedlings weed-free and thin out to prevent overcrowding; alternatively, sow seeds in clumps 4-6 in (10-15 cm) apart for a good mass of color.*

Linaria maroccana 'Fairy Bouquet'

LOBELIA

Native to temperate regions, particularly of the Americas and Africa, this large genus consists of 370 species of annuals, perennials and shrubs. They inhabit marshes, meadows, woodlands, deserts— even mountain slopes. All have neat foliage and brightly colored flowers. They vary in growth habit from low bedding types to tall, herbaceous perennials or shrubs, and they are suitable for edging, containers, hanging baskets and rock gardens. Some are suited to wild gardens or sites near water.

CULTIVATION Frost-hardy to somewhat frost-tender, these plants grow best in well-drained, moist, light loam enriched with animal manure or compost. Most grow in sun or part-shade and prefer dry winter conditions. Fertilize weekly with a liquid manure during flowering, and prune after the first flowers fade to encourage a

Lobelia erinus 'Crystal Palace'

second flush. Propagate annuals from seed in spring, perennial species from seed or by division in spring or fall (autumn), and perennial cultivars by division only. Transplant from late fall (autumn) until early spring.

Lobelia erinus
Edging lobelia

This tufted, often semi-trailing, compact annual is native to South Africa. It is slow growing, and reaches a height of only 4-8 in (10–20 cm) and spread of 4-6 in (10–15 cm). It has dense, oval to lanceolate leaves which taper at the base and it bears small, 2-lipped pinkish purple flowers continuously from spring to early fall (autumn). 'Cambridge Blue' (deep blue), 'Colour Cascade' (blue, violet, pink and white) and the dwarf 'Crystal Palace' (deep violet-blue) are popular.

ZONES 7–11.

Lobelia erinus 'Colour Cascade'

LOBULARIA

Frost hardy, dwarf plants, the 5 species of annuals and perennials in this genus suit rockeries, window boxes and borders. All are native to the Mediterranean and the Canary Islands; the annuals are the most popular. The tiny, 4-petalled, fragrant flowers appear in compact, terminal racemes in summer and early fall (autumn).

CULTIVATION They require full sun and fertile, well-drained soil. Deadhead regularly to encourage continuous flowering. Propagate from seed in spring or, if outdoors, from late spring to fall (autumn).

Lobularia maritima
syn. *Alyssum maritimum*
Sweet alyssum, sweet Alice

Popular for its masses of tiny, honey-scented white, lilac, pink or violet flowers which bloom over a long season, from spring to early fall (autumn), this spreading annual is a good choice for edging, rock gardens or window boxes. It has a low, rounded compact habit and it rapidly achieves a height of 3-12 in (8–30 cm) and a spread of 8-12 in (20–30 cm). **'Violet Queen'** is the darkest garden variety.

ZONES 7–10.

Lobularia maritima

Lobularia maritima

LUNARIA

Honesty

The origin of the common name for this genus of 3 species of annuals, biennials and perennials is uncertain. They are allied to stocks (*Matthiola*) and perhaps best known for their silvery, dried seed pods. Sprays of honesty have been popular as dried flower arrangements since the eighteenth century.

CULTIVATION Plant in full sun or part-shade in fertile, moist but well-drained soil. Propagate biennials from seed and perennials from seed or by division in fall (autumn) or spring. They self-seed quite readily.

Lunaria annua
syn. *Lunaria biennis*

This native of southern Europe and the Mediterranean coast is worth growing for its attractive flowers and seed pods. It flowers throughout spring and early summer, bearing heads of fragrant, 4-petalled, rosy magenta, white or violet-purple flowers. Its leaves are

Useful Tip

Lunaria annua *self-seeds readily, so you can merely sit back and wait for the new plants to appear in spring.*

pointed, oval, serrated and bright green. The circular seed pods are silvery and almost translucent. Erect in habit, this biennial grows to a height of 30 in (75 cm) and a spread of 12 in (30 cm).

ZONES 8–10.

LUPINUS

Lupin, lupine

These legumes are grown for their long, erect spikes of showy pea-flowers which come in a range of colors. In addition, they are used as animal fodder, their nitrogen-fixing properties make them valuable as 'green manure', and a few species are even grown for grain, for consumption by both humans and livestock. The genus comprises 200 species of annuals, perennials, semi-evergreen and evergreen shrubs and subshrubs, most of them from North America, southern Europe and North Africa. Unlike other legumes, which have pinnate leaves, the compound leaves of the lupin are palmate, with 5 or more leaflets radiating from a common stalk. Flowers may be blue, purple, pink, white, yellow, orange or red.

CULTIVATION Plant them in full sun in well-drained, moderately fertile, slightly acidic, sandy soil. Most prefer cool wet winters and long dry summers, although they need lots of water in the growing season and should be mulched in

Lunaria annua

dry regions. Remove spent flowers to prolong plant life and to prevent self-seeding. Propagate species from seed in fall (autumn).

Useful Tip

Lupins do not need a very fertile soil, and too much nitrogen in particular will favor excessive foliage, at the expense of flowers.

Lupinus hartwegii
Hairy lupin

This fast growing Mexican annual is compact and erect, reaching 30 in (75 cm) in height and 15 in (38 cm) in spread. Its leaves are hairy and dark green, and in late winter, spring and early summer it produces slender spikes of abundant blue, white or pink flowers.

ZONES 7–11.

Lupinus hartwegii

M

MATTHIOLA

Stock, gillyflower

Very few of the some 55 species of annuals, biennials and subshrubby perennials in this genus are grown in gardens apart from *Matthiola longipetala* subsp. *bicornis* (the night-scented stock) and the *M. incana* cultivars. They grow wild in North Africa, Europe and central and southwestern Asia. The leaves are usually gray-green and the perfumed flowers can be produced from spring to fall (autumn). Although they are good as both bedding plants and cut flowers, stocks are vulnerable to pests like cabbage root fly and diseases including downy mildew, club-root and gray mold.

CULTIVATION Plant in a sunny site in moist but well-drained, neutral or alkaline soil. Stake the taller plants and protect all from strong winds. In spring, propagate from seed sown *in situ* at staggered intervals, for night-scented stock, or sown in seed trays, for *M. incana*.

Matthiola incana

Best grown as an annual, this frost-hardy, bushy plant is well-loved for its fragrant single or double flowers. It can reach a height of 24 in (60 cm) with a spread of 12 in (30 cm). The lance-shaped leaves are gray-green and 3–6 in (8–15 cm) spikes of flowers in shades of pink, purple, red or white are borne in spring. Many

Matthiola incana

cultivars are available. '**Mammoth Column**' may be 30 in (75 cm) tall, and produces a single, 12-15 in (30–38 cm) spike of mixed or separate colors.

ZONES 6–10.

MESEMBRYANTHEMUM

Ice plant, pig face

Although it once included most of the so-called ice plants (those small succulents with daisy-like flowers), *Mesembryanthemum* now comprises only a few species of creeping or prostrate succulent annuals or biennials from South Africa. These are characterized by leaves covered with glistening, swollen surface cells, which give the plants a crystalline appearance. The small flowers are white, pink or red, very rarely yellow. In California and Australia, where they were grown as ornamentals, they have naturalized.

CULTIVATION Intolerant of all but the lightest frost, they need very light soil and full sun at all times. Propagate from seed in spring.

Mesembryanthemum crystallinum

This is the best known species of the *Mesembryanthemum* genus. It is an annual, carpet-forming succulent that grows 4 in (10 cm) high.

Mesembryanthemum crystallinum

It has dense, flat leaves with undulating edges. The small, shiny papillae (glands) covering the leaves, flower stems and cups glisten in the sun. Groups of 3–5 white, narrow-petalled flowers 1 in (25 mm) wide appear in summer.

ZONES 9–11.

MOLUCCELLA

Despite the name, none of the 4 annual and short-lived perennial species in this genus grow wild in the Moluccas; instead, they are distributed from northwestern India west towards the eastern Mediterranean. Only the annuals, which are tall, branched plants with fragrant white flowers and attractive green calyces, are commonly cultivated. Plants may be 3 ft (1 m) tall or more and have toothed leaves.

CULTIVATION Marginally frost hardy, these undemanding plants need only full sun and moderately fertile, moist but well-drained soil. Propagate from seed sown *in situ* in fall (autumn) or spring.

Moluccella laevis
Bells of Ireland, Irish green bellflower, Molucca balm, shell flower

A fairly fast growing, branching annual which grows to a height of

Moluccella laevis

3 ft (1 m) and spread of 12 in (30 cm), this summer-flowering plant is native to Turkey, Syria and the Caucasus. It has rounded, pale green leaves and flower spikes which have distinctive shell-like, apple-green calyces; the white flowers within are tiny and insignificant. They make good cut flowers.

ZONES 7–10.

Useful Tip

Whether in the garden or arranged, dried or fresh, in a tall vase, the unusual calyces of Molucca laevis *make a stunning display.*

MONARDA

Bergamot, horsemint, bee balm

The leaves and flowers of bergamot are used medicinally, and to flavor teas and add scent to potpourris; the flowers are valued both for their beauty and their fragrance. This is a North American genus of 15 species of annuals and perennials with green, sometimes purple-tinged, veined, aromatic leaves and 2-lipped, tubular flowers from mid-summer to early fall (autumn). Plants may be sparsely branching, or single-stemmed.

CULTIVATION These plants are very frost hardy and best planted in full sun although they will toler-ate some shade. Annuals do best in sandy soil, perennials like moist soil; all need well-drained soil. Propagate annuals from seed sown *in situ*, perennials by division.

Monarda citriodora
Lemon mint

This annual from central and southern USA and northern Mexico has beautiful, scented flowers: curved and tubular and usually white, pink or purplish, with a hairy mouth. The plant grows to 24 in (60 cm) tall.

ZONES 5–11.

Monarda citriodora

MYOSOTIS

Forget-me-not

The botanical name *Myosotis*, from the Greek for 'mouse ear', refers to the pointed leaves; the common name derives from their traditional association with love and loyalty. This genus comprises 50 or more annuals and perennials, including 34 New Zealand natives; the most widely grown are those from the temperate Europe, Asia and the Americas. Most species are good in rock gardens and borders, or as ground cover beneath trees and shrubs. The blue (or pink or white) flowers are dainty and bloom in spring. The plants fade after flowering.

CULTIVATION Mostly quite frost hardy, these trouble-free plants do best in semi-shade or a sunny spot with protection by larger plants. Plant in fertile, well-drained soil, and apply fertilizer before the flowering period. Propagate from seed in fall (autumn)—once established, they self-seed freely.

Useful Tip

Spray plants affected by powdery mildew with a solution of one teaspoon each of clean dishwashing water and baking soda per litre, and repeat weekly.

Myosotis sylvatica

Myosotis sylvatica
Garden forget-me-not

Usually grown as an annual, this European biennial or short-lived perennial is loved for its bright lavender-blue, yellow-eyed flowers which appear in spring and early summer. It forms tufts of hairy foliage 18 in (45 cm) high and 12 in (30 cm) wide. Many named selections exist, some more compact, some pink

Useful Tip

If you want to help garden beds retain moisture, lay mulch to a depth of about 3 in (7 cm) before the dry weather begins, and top it up each year as necessary.

or white. **'Blue Ball'** is good for edging.

ZONES 5–10.

Myosotis sylvatica 'Blue Ball'

NO

NEMESIA

Nemesia grows wild in sandy soils near the coast, or scrubby, often disturbed, soils inland in South Africa. The genus consists of 50-odd species of annuals, perennials and subshrubs. The showy, 2-lipped, trumpet-shaped flowers are borne singly in the upper leaf axils or in terminal racemes. The leaves are opposite and simple. The flowering period is short, but cutting back hard when flowering starts to slow will encourage a second flush.

Nemesia strumosa

CULTIVATION Intolerant of extremes of heat and humidity, these plants prefer a protected, sunny aspect and fertile, well-drained soil. Pinch out growing shoots on young plants to promote bushiness. Propagate from seed in early fall (autumn) or early spring in cool areas.

Nemesia strumosa

A popular bedding plant for its colorful spring flowers, it is a fast growing, bushy annual which grows to a height of 8-12 in (20–30 cm) and a spread of 10 in (25 cm). It has lance-shaped, pale green leaves which are often toothed and bears large yellow, white, red or orange blooms on short terminal racemes. Cultivars include the compact **'Blue Gem'** (small, clear blue flowers) and **'Prince of Orange'** (orange flowers with a purple blotch) and the bicolored **'Red and White'**.

ZONES 9–11.

Nemesia strumosa 'Blue Gem'

NEMOPHILA

The vivid, open, 5-petalled blooms—mostly blue—of these 11 annual species are characteristic. They are ideal as border edging and are also excellent for containers. These natives of western USA flower in spring and summer.

CULTIVATION They grow well in full sun or part-shade in friable, moisture-retentive soil. Choose a site sheltered from winds and damage by passers-by. Water well to help prolong blooming. Propagate from seed sown *in situ* in fall (autumn); they self-seed freely. Check for aphids.

Nemophila maculata
Five spot

Each of the veined, white petals has a prominent deep purple spot at its tip, hence the common name. This species is grown in massed plantings for its prolonged summer flowering period and its ferny foliage. It grows to 12 in (30 cm) tall.

ZONES 7–11.

Nemophila maculata

NICOTIANA

Flowering tobacco

The commercial tobacco plant is a member of this American and Australian genus which comprises 67 species of annuals, biennials, perennials and shrubs in all. Other species are grown in gardens for the fragrance of their tubular to trumpet-shaped flowers, which usually open at night (those of modern strains remain open all day, but are less fragrant). The plants are sticky to the touch, but make good cut flowers.

CULTIVATION Plant these marginally frost hardy to frost tender plants in full sun or light shade and fertile, moist but well-drained soil. Propagate from seed in early spring. Check for snails and caterpillars.

Nicotiana alata
syn. *Nicotiana affinis*

A short-lived perennial—often grown as an annual—it flowers through summer and early fall (autumn), bearing clusters of flowers in white, red or shades of pink. The flowers open towards evening and release their scent on warm, still nights. Rosette forming, it has oval leaves and grows to a height of about 3 ft (1 m) with a spread of 12 in (30 cm).

ZONES 7–11.

Nicotiana alata

Nicotiana langsdorfii

Nicotiana langsdorfii

This summer-flowering, sticky, branching annual grows to 5 ft (1.5 m) tall. The flowers are fine, tubular and apple-green and are borne in abundance. If conditions are favorable, they will readily self-seed.

ZONES 9–11.

NIGELLA

This genus of about 15 annual species is native to the Mediterranean and western Asia. It is grown for its flowers and decorative, sometimes inflated seed pods which look attractive in both fresh and dried flower arrangements.

CULTIVATION Plant in full sun in fertile, well-drained soil and deadhead to prolong flowering (unless you want the seed pods). Propagate from seed sown *in situ* in fall (autumn) or spring; the seedlings resent being transplanted. They will self-seed if allowed.

Nigella damascena

Nigella damascena
Love-in-a-mist, devil-in-a-bush

A particularly attractive plant, bearing spurred, many-petalled, pale to lilac-blue or white flowers in spring and early summer, this annual is fully frost-hardy. The flowers nestle within the bright green, feathery foliage and are followed by rounded, green seed pods that mature to brown. It grows rapidly to 24 in (60 cm) tall, with a spread of 8 in (20 cm). **'Miss Jekyll'** is a double blue form.

ZONES 6–10.

Nolana paradoxa

NOLANA

A group of 18 species of erect to spreading annuals, perennials and subshrubs make up this genus from Chile, Peru and the Galapagos Islands. Most are no more than 8 in (20 cm) tall, although they may spread to 18 in (45 cm) or more. The elliptical leaves are 1-2 ½ in (2.5–6 cm) long, bright green and may be slightly succulent. The flowers are up to 1 ½ in (35 mm) in diameter, broadly trumpet-shaped and are carried singly or in small clusters throughout the growing season. The flowers are usually white to purple with yellow throats. They are suitable for borders, ground covers or hanging baskets, depending on their growth habit.

CULTIVATION They tolerate only the lightest frosts. Grow in humus-rich, well-drained soil in sun or part-shade. Pinch stem tips back to promote bushiness. Propagate from seed, layers or tip cuttings.

Nolana paradoxa

Grow this creeping annual as ground cover, or in hanging baskets or containers, in full sun. It reaches only 10 in (25 cm) in height and 15 in (38 cm) in width, but over the summer produces an abundance of purple-blue flowers, each with a pronounced white throat. Many hybrids exist: **'Blue Bird'** has deep blue and white flowers.

ZONES 8–11.

OCIMUM

Basil

This genus comprises some 35 species of fairly frost-tender annuals, perennials and shrubs native to tropical Asia and Africa. They are widely cultivated in many other countries for their highly aromatic leaves, which are used for medicinal purposes or to flavor salads, soups, sauces, stews and curries. Their leaves are generally oval and are borne in opposite pairs. In late summer, the small, tubular flowers are borne in whorls towards the ends of the stems. They have small to large, often colorful, bracts.

CULTIVATION Ocimums thrive in a protected, warm, sunny site and they prefer a moist but well-drained soil. Pinch back plants regularly to encourage bushiness and to prevent them going to seed quickly. Propagate from seed in mid-spring. Protect from late frosts and check for chewing insects and snails.

Ocimum basilicum
Basil, sweet basil

This is the basil so well-loved by cooks. A native of tropical Asia, sweet basil is not only the most commonly grown and most widely used basil, but one of the most widely used herbs in Mediter-

ranean cooking. Although the fresh leaves give the best results, they may be frozen for use in winter (they lose their flavor when dried). This tender annual grows to about 18 in (45 cm), and it has light green, oval leaves with a spicy, clove-like aroma. Small white flowers are carried in whorls towards the ends of the stems in late summer. A number of varieties include a compact small leaf type; a crinkled, lettuce leaf variety and the beautiful 'Dark Opal', which has rich purple stems and leaves. Perennial varieties exist, but have an inferior flavor. The tiny leaves of the dwarf 'Minimum' are used in the Greek Orthodox Church for sprinkling holy water. In cooler climates, grow basil as a summer annual.

ZONES 10-12.

Ocimum species, including *O. basilicum*

OENOTHERA

Evening primrose

The seeds of *Oenothera biennis* yield evening primrose oil which contains certain fatty acids said to be beneficial to health if consumed regularly in modest quantities. *Oenothera* consists of more than 120 species of annuals, biennials and perennials originally from temperate regions of both North and South America but widely naturalized elsewhere. In summer, their delicate flowers—each with 4 petals and a long basal tube—open at dawn or dusk and fade rapidly. They may be yellow, red, white or (less commonly) pink. Most species are pollinated by nocturnal insects and only release their fragrance at night; the flowers of some do not even open during the day.

CULTIVATION Mostly frost hardy, these plants grow best in a well-drained, sandy soil in an open, sunny site. They will tolerate dry conditions. Propagate from seed or by division in spring or fall (autumn), or from softwood cuttings in late spring.

Oenothera biennis
Common evening primrose

This erect, fast growing, hairy biennial bears tall spikes of large, scented yellow flowers which open in the evening and fade before noon. It flowers from summer to fall (autumn) and grows to a height of 5 ft (1.5 m).

ZONES 4–10.

Useful Tip

Plant Oenothera biennis *outside near windows and patio doors and in summer you will enjoy wafts of fragrance in the evening air.*

Oenothera biennis

PR

PAPAVER

Poppy

The flowers of this genus begin as nodding buds which open skywards into wide, cup-shaped blooms, and are followed by characteristic seed pods like pepperpots. Around 50 annual, biennial or perennial species make up the genus, mainly from the temperate parts of Eurasia and Africa, with a couple from eastern USA.

Romneya (the tree poppy), *Eschscholzia* (the Californian poppy) and *Meconopsis* (the blue poppy) are all related.

CULTIVATION Fully frost hardy, they like deep, moist, well-drained soil and little or no shade. Sow seed in spring or fall (autumn); many species self-seed readily.

Papaver rhoeas, Shirley Series

Papaver commutatum

A massed planting of these bright red summer flowers gives a spectacular result reminiscent of a Monet masterpiece. This annual is related to blood red *Papaver rhoeas*. The stems are hairy.

ZONES 8–10.

Papaver nudicaule
Iceland poppy

Although a perennial, this popular tuft-forming species from North America and Asia Minor is almost invariably grown as an annual, in rock gardens and for cutting. It is winter- and spring-flowering, the large, fragrant, crinkled flowers available in white, yellow, orange or pink. The leaves are pale green, and the stems are long and hairy. It grows 12-24 in (30–60 cm) tall with a 6-8 in (15–20 cm) spread.

ZONES 2–10.

Papaver rhoeas
Corn poppy, field poppy, Flanders poppy

This fast growing annual from Asia Minor has small and delicate, single, scarlet flowers with a black

Papaver commutatum

Papaver nudicaule

central cross; the cultivated varieties (**Shirley Series**) come in reds, pinks, whites and bicolors and have a pale center. The leaves are pale green and lobed. Plants grow to 24 in (60 cm) high with a 12 in (30 cm) spread. Double-flowered strains are also available. **'Mother of Pearl'** has gray, pink or blue-purple flowers.

ZONES 5–9.

Useful Tip

Plants which bear single flowers may be 'lost' unless planted in a group; two examples being Papaver commutatum *and* P. rhoeas, *which are stunning when grown* en masse.

PETUNIA

The some 35 species of annuals, biennials and shrubby perennials in this genus are native to South America. *'Petun'* means 'tobacco' in a local Indian dialect, and petunias are indeed relatives of *Nicotiana*, their leaves having a similar narcotic effect. The dark green leaves are hairy and smooth-edged and the fluted, trumpet-shaped flowers are white, purple, red, blue, pink or mixed. Intensive breeding for many years has concentrated almost exclusively on *Petunia* x *hybrida*. Garden petunias, always grown as annuals, are popular worldwide as bedding plants and for containers of all kinds.

Petunia x *hybrida* cultivar

CULTIVATION Frost-tender and fairly fast growing, they like well-drained, fertile soil and a sunny site; they thrive where summers are hot. Flowers of the larger Grandiflora hybrids may be easily rain-damaged, but others, mainly the Multiflora hybrids, are more resilient; they all need shelter from wind. Sow seed under glass in early spring, or buy seedlings and plant in early summer. Fertilize monthly until flowering is established; deadhead regularly. Pinch back hard to encourage branching. Watch for cucumber mosaic and tomato spotted wilt.

Petunia x hybrida

Garden petunias are divided into 4 groups of cultivars and seedling strains: the **Grandiflora** petunias (sprawling plants with scattered, very wide, shallow flowers) and **Multiflora** petunias (more compact, with masses of smaller blooms), both reaching about 12 in (30 cm) in height; the **Nana Compacta** petunias (less than 6 in [15 cm] high, with profuse small flowers) and the **Pendula** petunias (prostrate, trailing plants ideal for hanging baskets). The popular Grandifloras have a huge range of newer F1 hybrids including the **Cascade** and **Supercascade Series** (or Magic Series) and '**Giants of California**'. The Multifloras include the **Plum, Bonanza, Celebrity** (including '**Pink Morn**') and **Madness Series** ('**Purple Wave**').

ZONES 9–11.

Petunia x *hybrida*, Madness Series 'Purple Wave'

PHACELIA

Scorpion weed

This is a genus of around 150 species of generally shrubby annuals, biennials and perennials native to the Americas. They range from 6 in (15 cm) to over 5 ft (1.5 m) tall. The young shoots and leaves are sometimes downy and the leaves are often toothed or lobed, even pinnate. They bear clusters of small 5-petalled flowers, usually in blue or purple shades, often with white centers. Annual species are suitable for wild gardens and borders; their nectar-rich blooms attract bees and other insects.

CULTIVATION Fully frost hardy, they are generally easy to grow in any light but moist, well-drained soil in full sun. Propagate annuals and biennials from seed, perennials from seed or cuttings.

Phacelia grandiflora

This 3 ft (1 m) annual from southern California has serrated-edged, elliptical leaves and bears mauve to white flowers which are 1½ in (35mm) wide.

ZONES 8–11.

Useful Tip

Dig spent Phacelia *plants into the soil; they are useful as* 'green manure'.

Phacelia grandiflora

PHLOX

These are some of the brightest of the summer flowers; the botanical name, meaning 'flame', is highly appropriate. The genus comprises more than 60 species of evergreen and semi-evergreen annuals and perennials, most of them native to North America. The abundant flowers are both fragrant and showy, making phlox popular for borders and bedding displays.

CULTIVATION The annuals grow in almost any climate; perennials are easily grown in any temperate climate and need a lot of water. Plant in full sun or semi-shade, in fertile, moist but well-drained soil. Propagate from seed or cuttings or by division. Red spider mite, eelworm and powdery mildew can be a problem.

Phlox drummondii
Annual phlox

A fast growing, bushy annual growing to 15 in (38 cm) in height and half that in spread, this is a good bedding plant for summer and fall (autumn) color. It bears closely clustered, small, flattish flowers with 5 petals in reds, pinks, purples and creams. It has lanceolate, light green leaves and is frost hardy. **'Sternenzauber'** (syn. 'Twinkle') has star-shaped flowers with pointed petals. Dwarf strains grow only to 4 in (10 cm).

ZONES 6–10.

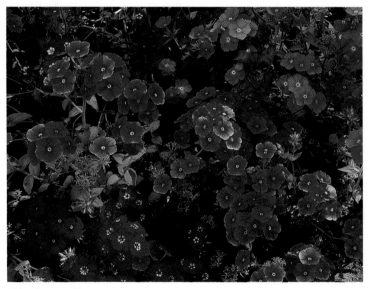

Phlox drummondii

PORTULACA

This genus, from the warm, dry regions of the world, comprises about 100 species of semi-succulent annuals or perennials. They are popular for their small, rose-like flowers in white, yellow, apricot, pink, purple or scarlet which bloom best in dry summers. The fleshy leaves are attractive too, varying from white to green or red.

CULTIVATION Easy to grow in all climates. In cooler areas, plant out only when the danger of frost is passed. They need sun, well-drained soil and only occasional watering. Propagate from seed in spring or cuttings in summer. Check for aphids.

Portulaca grandiflora
Rose moss, sun plant

This spreading species, one of the few annual succulents, is native to South America. It grows 8 in (20 cm) high and spreads to 6 in (15 cm). The small, lanceolate, fleshy, bright green leaves lie like beads on their reddish stems. The summer flowers are large, open and usually double; they are 3 in (8 cm) wide and bright yellow, pink, red or orange. The flowers close at night and on dull days. It is suitable as a ground cover or in a rockery or border.

ZONES 10–11.

Portulaca grandiflora

PRIMULA
Primrose

About 400 species belong in this genus which is distributed throughout the temperate regions of the northern hemisphere, mainly in China and the Himalayas. They also grow wild on high mountains in the tropics, as far south as Papua New Guinea. Although most are rhizomatous, the rhizomes of some are poorly developed, and these species are short lived. The leaves tend to be broadest toward their tips, with toothed or scalloped margins and they often form a basal tuft or rosette. The flowering stems vary in form: most carry successive whorls or a single umbel of flowers; some bear flowers on a terminal head or short spike; others, singly or in small groups on short stalks. Flower shape, size and color

Primula malacoides

vary widely, but generally, flowers are tubular, opening into a funnel or flat disc with at least 5 petals, often notched at the tips.

CULTIVATION They thrive in fertile, well-drained soil and they like part-shade and ample water. Deadhead and trim back foliage after flowering. Propagate from seed in spring, early summer or fall (autumn), by division or from root cuttings.

Primula malacoides
Fairy primrose

This frost-tender perennial from China is always grown as a spring-flowering annual. Single or double flowers bloom in spiral masses, ranging from white to pink to magenta. The oval leaves and erect stem are hairy. It reaches a height and spread of 12 in (30 cm) or more.

ZONES 8–11.

RESEDA
Mignonette

Mignonette used to be a favorite with perfumers and the plant is still cultivated in France for its essential oils; gardeners love it more for its

Reseda odorata

spicy scent than its small yellow-orange flowers. The genus originates in Asia, Africa and Europe and contains about 60 species of erect or spreading, branching annuals and perennials. The star-shaped, greenish white or greenish yellow flowers appear in spike-like racemes from spring to fall (autumn). They are attractive to bees.

CULTIVATION Plant in full sun or part-shade in well-drained, fertile, preferably alkaline soil. Deadhead to prolong flowering. Propagate from seed in late winter.

Reseda odorata
Common mignonette

The flowers of this reasonably fast growing annual from North Africa have a pungent aroma. The tiny greenish or white to reddish green flowers have dark orange stamens and are borne in conical heads from summer to early fall (autumn). The plants grow to 24 in (60 cm) high and about half that in spread.

ZONES 6–10.

RUDBECKIA
Coneflower,
marmalade daisy

The rudbeckias have bright, daisy-like, composite flowers with prominent central cones reminiscent of *Echinacea*, which explains the shared common name. The genus includes about 15 species of annuals, biennials and perennials from the moist meadows and light woodlands of North America. The single, double or semi-double flowers are usually in tones of yellow, and the cones range from green through rust, to purple and black. Plants may vary in height from 24 in (60 cm) to as much as 10 ft (3 m). Some species are grown as cut flowers.

CULTIVATION Moderately to fully frost hardy, these plants prefer full sun or part-shade and like moisture-retentive, loamy soil. Propagate from seed or by division in spring or fall (autumn). Aphids may be a problem.

Rudbeckia hirta
Black-eyed Susan

The common name derives from the purplish brown central 'eye' of these bright yellow flowers. This biennial or short-lived perennial, often grown as an annual, has lanceolate, mid-green, hairy leaves and flowers in summer to fall (autumn). It reaches 12-36 in (30–90 cm) tall, with a spread of 12 in (30 cm). **'Irish Eyes'** has olive green centers and **'Marmalade'** has large golden flowers. Dwarf cultivars are usually treated as annuals.

ZONES 3–10.

Rudbeckia hirta

ST

Salpiglossis

These natives of the southern Andes can be challenging to grow, but in mild climates with cool summers, they can be very rewarding. Their petunia-like flowers come in rich tones of crimson, scarlet, orange, blue, purple and white, all veined and laced with gold. Two species of annuals and perennials are suitable for borders or as greenhouse plants in cold climates.

Salpiglossis sinuata

CULTIVATION They like full sun in rich, well-drained soil. Deadhead regularly. Sow seed in early spring *in situ*: seedlings do not like to be transplanted. Check for aphids.

Salpiglossis sinuata
Painted tongue

Flowering in summer and early fall (autumn), this frost-tender annual from Peru and Argentina is a colorful asset in the garden. The trumpet-shaped, veined flowers are 2 in (5 cm) wide and may be red, orange, yellow, blue or purple; the lanceolate leaves are light green. It grows rapidly, to reach a height of 18-24 in (45–60 cm) and a spread of at least 15 in (38 cm). It dislikes dry conditions.

ZONES 8–11.

Salvia

Sage

Salvia officinalis, the common sage, is said to be a tonic and good

for sore throats and *Salvia*, derived from the Latin *salvus* meaning 'safe' or 'well', is probably a reference to this. The aromatic leaves of some species are grown as a herb used in stuffing and as part of the *bouquet garni*, but even these plants are attractive. This, the largest genus of the mint family, consists of about 900 species of annuals, perennials and soft-wooded shrubs, represented in most parts of the world except very cold regions and tropical rainforests. The tubular, 2-lipped flowers are very distinctive, the lower lip being flat and the upper lip forming a helmet or boat shape; the 2-lipped calyx may also be colored. The flower colors include some of the brightest blues and scarlets of any plants, though yellow is rare.

CULTIVATION Sages tend to do best planted in full sun in well-drained, light-textured soil with adequate watering in summer. Most of the shrubby Mexican and South American species will tolerate only light frosts, although some perennials are reasonably frost hardy. Propagate from seed in spring, cuttings in early summer, or by division of rhizomatous species at almost any time. Snails, slugs and caterpillars attack many *Salvia* species.

Salvia splendens 'Van Houttei'

Salvia splendens
Scarlet sage

This Brazilian species, grown as an annual, bears dense terminal spikes of scarlet flowers from summer to early fall (autumn). The leaves are toothed and elliptical. It grows 3–4 ft (1–1.2 m) tall and wide. Provide some shade in hotter climates; it is moderately frost hardy. Cultivars **'Salsa Burgundy'** (deep burgundy flowers) and **'Van Houttei'** (deep red calyx with large lighter red flowers) both need a little shade. **ZONES 9–12.**

Useful Tip

Although most often grown as an annual, if left to grow, scarlet sage will make a bushy plant.

SANVITALIA
Creeping zinnia

These 7 species of annuals and short-lived perennials from southwestern USA and Mexico are members of the daisy family. The oval leaves are paired and the small white or yellow flowers have a dark purplish black or white center. They are grown as annuals and make good ground covers, rock garden plants and hanging basket specimens.

CULTIVATION They thrive in full sun in humus-rich, well-drained soil. Propagate from seed sown *in situ* or in small pots; avoid root disturbance when replanting.

Sanvitalia procumbens

This summer-flowering, fully frost-hardy annual from Mexico bears a profusion of bright yellow, 1 in (25 mm), daisy-like flowerheads with blackish centers. A prostrate species with mid-green, oval leaves, it grows to 8 in (20 cm) high and spreads at least 15 in (38 cm). **ZONES 7–11.**

Sanvitalia procumbens

SCABIOSA

Scabious, pincushion flower

This genus of 80 annuals, biennials and perennials from sunny sites, dry slopes and meadows in temperate climates (mainly in the Mediterranean, but also the rest of Europe, Africa, Asia and Japan), bears tall-stemmed, honey-scented flowers ideal for cutting. The blooms, which have multiple florets and protruding filaments giving a pincushion effect, range from white, yellow, red, blue and mauve to deep purple. Annual species are excellent for borders; perennials suit wildflower gardens or rock gardens.

CULTIVATION Thrive in full sun in well-drained, alkaline soil. Propagate annuals from seed in spring and perennials from cuttings in summer, seed in fall (autumn) or by division in early spring.

Scabiosa anthemifolia

Scabiosa anthemifolia

This is a South African annual or short-lived perennial with arching stems up to 30 in (75 cm) long, which bears 2½ in (6 cm) flowers in shades of mauve, violet or rose.

ZONES 7–11.

SCHIZANTHUS

Poor man's orchid, butterfly flower

These 12 to 15 species of spring-flowering annuals from the mountains of Chile are both colorful and adaptable. The flowers come in shades of pink, mauve, red, purple and white, all with gold-speckled throats; they resemble small orchids but are related instead to *Petunia*. Plants grow to about 3 ft (1 m) high and 12 in (30 cm) wide. Most garden plants are hybrids.

CULTIVATION They do not tolerate extremes of heat or cold, growing best in a mild, frost-free

Useful Tip

Schizanthus is very adaptable—it is ideal for containers or hanging baskets beneath trees and will grow in the garden as long as it is sheltered from the midday heat.

Schizanthus x *wisetonensis*

climate; in colder climates, grow them in a greenhouse. Plant in full sun in fertile, well-drained soil and pinch out growing tips of young plants to promote bushiness. Propagate from seed in summer or fall (autumn).

Schizanthus x wisetonensis

Most garden strains derive from this erect species which flowers from spring to summer, bearing tubular to flared, 2-lipped flowers in white, blue, pink or reddish brown, often flushed with yellow. It has lanceolate, light green leaves and grows to 18 in (45 cm) high with a spread of 12 in (30 cm).

ZONES 7–11.

Useful Tip

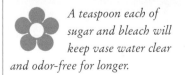

A teaspoon each of sugar and bleach will keep vase water clear and odor-free for longer.

SENECIO

Some 1000 species from all over the world make up this huge genus of plants ranging from annuals, biennials and perennials to evergreen tree-like shrubs and climbers, some of the species being succulent. The daisy-like flowers are usually yellow but sometimes red, orange, blue or purple and are clustered at the top of the plant. Some species contain alkaloids which are poisonous. The annuals are grown as bedding or container plants, the perennials as rock garden or border specimens.

CULTIVATION Varying from frost-tender to fully frost-hardy, these plants need reasonably fertile, well-drained soil and a sunny aspect. Prune tips to promote bushiness. Propagate annuals from seed in fall (autumn), perennials by division in spring and shrubs from cuttings in summer.

Senecio elegans

Senecio elegans
Wild cineraria

A South African native, this marginally frost-hardy, hairy annual has an erect habit, growing to 24 in (60 cm) tall. Its branching stems are covered with variable dark green leaves ranging from entire to pinnate, up to 3 in (8 cm) long. In spring to summer, daisy-like purplish pink flowers appear in dome-shaped terminal clusters. **ZONES 9–11.**

SILENE

Campion, catchfly

Some of the more than 500 species of annuals, biennials and deciduous or evergreen perennials in this genus exude gum from their stems. Flies get stuck to this, hence the name 'catchfly'. All the species, which are widely distributed throughout temperate and cold areas of the northern hemisphere, have 5-petalled flowers with notched or split petals, inflated calyces and small, elliptical, often silky leaves. Some suit being potted; others are good ground covers. The flowers of the weedier species may open only at night.

CULTIVATION Marginally to fully frost-hardy, these plants prefer fertile, well-drained soil and full or part-sun. Propagate from seed in spring or early fall (autumn) or from cuttings in spring.

Silene coeli-rosa
syns *Agrostemma coeli-rosa, Lychnis coeli-rosa, Viscaria elegans*
Rose of heaven

This is a summer-flowering, upright annual from the Mediterranean. It has pinkish purple flowers with deeply notched petals (good as cut flowers) and lanceolate, gray-green leaves. It grows rapidly to 18 in (45 cm) with a spread of 6 in (15 cm). **ZONES 6–11.**

Silene coeli-rosa

Useful Tip

Using liquid fertilizers is good water-saving practice, since unlike dry fertilizers, they do not take water from the soil.

SOLENOSTEMON

Coleus, flame nettle, painted nettle

This genus, comprising 60 species of low shrubby perennials, is native to tropical Africa and Asia. Species are grown for their colorful, often hairy, sometimes variegated, leaves. The stems are 4-angled and the opposite leaves are often toothed. Borne throughout the year, the tiny, tubular flowers may be blue, white or purple.

CULTIVATION Easy to grow in milder climates in humus-rich, moist but well-drained soil, as long as they have adequate summer moisture and shelter from hot sun. They are frost tender. Pinch back to promote bushiness. Propagate from seed or cuttings.

Solenostemon scutellarioides

syns *Coleus blumei* var. *verschaffeltii, C. scutellarioides*

This bushy, fast growing perennial from Southeast Asia is grown as an annual in more temperate climates. The serrated-edged leaves are a bright mixture of pink, green, red or yellow and shaped like a pointed oval. It grows 24 in (60 cm) high and 12 in (30 cm) across.

ZONES 10–12.

Solenostemon scutellaroides

STEIRODISCUS

A small South African genus comprising 5 annuals with toothed, divided leaves arranged in spirals. Yellow or orange daisy-like flowers appear in summer.

CULTIVATION They are frost tender, thriving in full sun and well-drained, humus-rich soil. Propagate from seed or cuttings.

Steirodiscus tagetes

The bright yellow or orange flowers are ¾ in (18 mm) wide and the divided leaves, 2 in (5 cm) long. This species grows to 12 in (30 cm) in height and has wiry, branching stems. **'Gold Rush'** is a larger yellow form.

ZONES 9–11.

Steirodiscus tagetes

SWAINSONA

Pea, desert pea

All but one of the some 50 species of perennials, annuals and sub-shrubs or trailing plants in this genus are endemic to Australia; one species comes from New Zealand. Most are found in dry to arid areas, although some prefer moister sites in cooler regions. The leaflets are mostly gray or gray-green, and the pea-shaped flowers, borne on extended racemes, range from white to blue, mauve and scarlet.

CULTIVATION Frost tender, they prefer full sun and moderately fertile, very well-drained soil. Propagate from seed or cuttings.

Swainsona formosa

Useful Tip

The best time to water your garden is first thing in the morning, before the temperature rises.

Swainsona formosa
syns *Clianthus dampieri,*
C. formosus
Sturt's desert pea

This slow growing, trailing annual grows wild in the dry Australian outback. Its small, grayish leaves show up its dramatic spring flowers, which are brilliant red with black-blotches. It grows to a height of 6 in (15 cm) and spread of 3 ft (1 m).

ZONES 9–11.

TAGETES

Marigold

Once rare, these fast growing annuals are now widely grown for their bright summer flowers which suit both borders and edging. They are also used as companion plants, since their roots are said to exude substances which keep pests at bay. Single or double flowers in orange, yellow, mahogany, brown and red contrast with deep green leaves; some have aromatic foliage.

CULTIVATION They thrive in full sun in fertile, well-drained soil in warm, frost-free climates, but in cooler climates, raise seedlings in a greenhouse. Deadhead regularly to prolong flowering. Propagate from seed in spring after the danger of frost has passed. They may be prone to attack by slugs, snails and botrytis.

Tagetes 'Disco Orange'

This cheerful, dwarf cultivar is ideal for the front of a summer border, and produces single, weather-resistant flowerheads from late spring to early fall (autumn).

ZONES 9–11.

Tagetes 'Disco Orange'

Tagetes patula

Tagetes patula
French marigold

'French' only because it was introduced to the gardening public via France from its native Mexico, this bushy annual rapidly reaches 12 in (30 cm) in height and spread. It flowers in summer and early fall (autumn), producing double carnation-like flowerheads in red, yellow and orange. The leaves are deep green and aromatic. Cultivars include **'Dainty Marietta'** (all-yellow single flowers); **'Naughty Marietta'** (single, golden yellow flowers with dark red-brown markings on the petal bases); and **'Honeycomb'** (large, mahogany-red flowers edged with gold).

ZONES 9–11.

THUNBERGIA

Named after the eighteenth-century Swedish botanist Dr Carl Peter Thunberg, this genus of over 90 species of mainly twining climbers and evergreen, clump-forming shrubs is native to Africa, Asia and Madagascar. They are grown for their showy, trumpet-shaped flowers of blue, orange, yellow, red or white, borne individually from the leaf axils or in trusses. The leaves are entire or lobed.

CULTIVATION Ranging from marginally frost hardy to frost tender, they prefer full sun (except during summer when they need part-shade and liberal water), and temperatures above 50°F (10°C).

Thunbergia alata

They will grow in any reasonably rich soil with adequate drainage. Support the stems and prune densely packed foliage during early spring. Propagate from seed in spring and cuttings in summer.

Thunbergia alata
Black-eyed Susan

This marginally frost hardy, climbing annual from tropical Africa will grow as a perennial in frost-free regions. Its deep green, cordate leaves are up to 3 in (8 cm) long and from early summer to fall (autumn) it produces a mass of 2 in (5 cm) wide orange flowers with black throats. It grows rapidly to 10 ft (3 m) tall. **ZONES 9–12.**

TITHONIA

Mexican sunflower

Ten species of mainly tall, somewhat woody annuals, biennials and perennials make up this genus from Central America and the West

Tithonia rotundifolia

Indies. As the common name suggests, they are related to sunflowers and bear large, bright yellow, orange or scarlet daisy-like flowerheads in summer and fall (autumn). The leaves are sharply lobed and their undersides are often hairy.

CULTIVATION Marginally frost hardy, these plants thrive in hot, dry conditions, but need lots of water. They like a site in full sun and prefer well-drained soil. Stake taller plants, deadhead regularly to encourage flowering and prune back hard after flowering to encourage new growth. Propagate from seed sown under glass in late winter or early spring.

Tithonia rotundifolia

Choose the site of this bulky annual with care: it can easily grow to 5 ft (1.5 m) tall with a spread of 3 ft (1 m). It bears large, 4 in (10 cm) wide, zinnia-like flowers in orange or scarlet; its leaves are heart-shaped. It makes long-lasting cut flowers. **'Torch'** has orange or red blooms and grows to 3 ft (1m).

ZONES 8–11.

Torenia fournieri

TORENIA

Wishbone flower

This genus of 40-50 species of erect to spreading, bushy annuals and perennials comes from tropical African and Asian woodlands. They have oval to lanceolate, entire or toothed, opposite leaves and in summer they bear racemes of trumpet-shaped, snapdragon-like flowers.

CULTIVATION Torenias prefer a warm, frost-free climate; in cooler climates, wait until all danger of frost has passed before planting out, or grow as potted plants in a greenhouse. They need fertile, well-drained soil in part-shade in a sheltered position. Pinch out the growing shoots of young plants to promote bushiness. Propagate from seed in spring.

Torenia fournieri
Bluewings

The ovate to elliptical, pale green leaves on this frost tender, branch-

Useful Tip

To conserve water: avoid watering the lawn, which will recover soon enough; control weeds, which use up valuable water; and choose plants suited to your climate.

ing annual have toothed edges. It grows fairly rapidly to a height of 12 in (30 cm) and a spread of 8 in (20 cm) and is suitable for a border or as a potted indoor plant. It flowers in summer and early fall (autumn), its blooms a deep purplish blue with a touch of yellow and pale in the center. Red, pink and white varieties are also available.

ZONES 9–12.

TROPAEOLUM

Nasturtium

The ever-popular nasturtium is valued for its brightly colored flowers and ease of cultivation. This genus from Chile and Mexico comprises 87 species of annuals, perennials and twining climbers. In warm climates, these plants self-sow freely, flower all year round and may survive for several years. The flowers, which may be single or double and are about 2 in (5 cm) across, come in red, orange, russet, yellow, cream—even blue. A white cultivar, bred in the nineteenth century, has since been lost.

CULTIVATION Varying from frost hardy to frost tender, most species prefer moist, well-drained soil in full sun or part-shade. Propagate from seed, basal stem cuttings or tubers in spring. Check for aphids and cabbage moth caterpillars.

Tropaeolum majus
Garden nasturtium,
Indian cress

The spicy-tasting leaves and flowers of this species are sometimes a colorful addition to salads. A vigorous, bushy annual with a climbing, sometimes scrambling habit, it has rounded leaves which are marked with radial veins.

It blooms in summer and fall (autumn); its 5-petalled flowers are spurred, open and trumpet-shaped, and come in many shades from deep red to pale yellow. It spreads to 3 ft (1 m) and reaches a height of up to 18 in (45 cm). Varieties exhibit single or double flowers and a compact or trailing habit; the **Alaska Hybrids** have variegated foliage and single flowers in a range of colors.

ZONES 8–11.

Tropaeolum majus, Alaska Hybrids

U-Z

URSINIA

Ursinias are native to southern Africa and Ethiopia and comprise up to 40 species of annuals, perennials, subshrubs and shrubs. They are grown mainly for their flowers: daisy-like, yellow, white, orange or occasionally red, with purple or yellow centers. A few are valued for their foliage, which is pinnate and fern-like, often downy and frequently aromatic.

CULTIVATION Varying from marginally frost hardy to frost tender, they require warm, dry climates, full sun and well-drained, moderately fertile soil. Propagate from cuttings or seed in spring. Protect from aphids.

Ursinia anethoides

A perennial usually grown as an annual, this summer-flowering species is bushy and evergreen. The leaves may be slightly hairy or hairless and the flowers, borne singly, are golden yellow. It grows up to 18 in (45 cm) tall and 14 in (35 cm) wide.

ZONES 9–11.

Ursinia anthemoides
Star of the veld

This bushy, frost-tender annual from South Africa has pale green, slightly hairy, scented foliage and it grows 15 in (38 cm) tall and 8 in (20 cm) wide. Flowers appear in summer and early fall (autumn), the flowerheads like orange-yellow daisies, each ray floret zoned with dark purple or copper in the center.

ZONES 9–11.

Top: *Ursinia anethoides*
Above: *Ursinia anthemoides*

VIOLA

Violet, heartsease, pansy

This is a huge genus of about 500 species of annuals, perennials and subshrubs, found in most temperate regions of the world including high mountains of the tropics, the majority being found in North America, the Andes and Japan. Most are creeping plants, either deciduous or evergreen, with slender to thick rhizomes and leaves usually kidney- or heart-shaped, though in some species they are divided into narrow lobes. In the wild, flowers are seldom more than 1 in (25 mm) across and characteristically have 3 spreading lower petals and 2 erect upper petals, with a short nectar spur projecting to the rear of the flower. Many species produce *cleistogamous* flowers, with smaller petals that do not open properly and able to set seed without cross-pollination. A few Eurasian species have been hybridized to produce garden pansies, violas and violettas with showy flowers in very bright or deep colors. Although these are almost always grown as annuals, some may be regarded as short-lived perennials.

CULTIVATION Most cultivated species tolerate light frosts at least and many are fully frost hardy. Pansies and violas *(Viola x wittrockiana)* are grown as annuals or pot plants in full sun and need shelter from drying winds. The perennial species suit rock gardens or ground covers beneath trees and taller shrubs, depending on their growth needs and habits. Propagate annuals with seed sown in late winter or early spring, under glass if necessary, planting out in late spring in soil that is well drained and not too rich. Water well and feed sparingly as flowers develop. Propagate perennial species by division or from cuttings.

Top: *Viola cornuta*
Above: *Viola tricolor* 'Bowles' Black'

Viola cornuta
Horned violet

One of the major parent species of pansies and violas, this spreading, rhizomatous evergreen is native to the Pyrenees and flowers in spring and summer. Each broad-faced flower has a short spur at the back; colors vary from pale blue to deep violet. Flowering stems arise from rhizomes and are up to 6 in (15 cm) long. **'Minor'** has smaller leaves and flowers.

ZONES 6–9.

Viola tricolor
Wild pansy, Johnny jump up, love-in-idleness

An annual, biennial or short-lived perennial well-known in Europe and temperate Asia, this species flowers in fall (autumn) and winter in mild climates if cut back in late summer. Neat flowers with appealing 'faces' come in shades of yellow, blue, violet and white. The oval to lanceolate leaves are lobed. It achieves a height and spread of 6 in (15 cm) and self-seeds readily. **'Bowles' Black'** has black velvety blooms with a yellow center.

ZONES 4–10.

Viola x *wittrockiana*
Pansy, viola

A well-deserving favorite in many gardens, these are colorful, compactly branched perennials almost always grown as biennials or annuals. It includes both pansies and violas, pansies traditionally characterized by the presence of dark blotches, but there are now intermediate types. Numerous cultivars bloom in late winter through spring and possibly into summer in cooler climates. The flowers, of many colors, are 2½–4 in (6–10 cm) across and have 5 petals; the mid-green leaves are elliptical and have shallow lobes. Plants grow slowly to about 8 in (20 cm) in height and spread. Pansy hybrids include the **Accord Series** (most colors, with a very dark blotch) and the **Imperial Series**, to which **'Lavender and Cherry'** belongs. Intermediate hybrids include the **Joker Series**, with contrasting colors such as orange and purple (**'Jolly Joker'**).

ZONES 5–10.

Viola x *wittrockiana* 'Imperial Lavender and Cherry'

XERANTHEMUM

Immortelle

Immortelles are so-called because their dried flowers retain their color for many years—they are 'immortal'. The genus consists of 5 or 6 annuals from the Mediterranean region as far as Iran. The daisy-like flowerheads are borne on long stems and the small, fertile flowers are surrounded by white, purple or pink papery bracts. The upright, branching stems have narrow, hoary leaves.

CULTIVATION Moderately frost hardy, they prefer a sunny aspect and fertile, well-drained soil. Propagate in spring from seed sown *in situ*.

Xeranthemum annuum
Immortelle

This summer-flowering annual produces heads of purple, daisy-like flowers in whites, pinks and mauves; a 'double' flower is also available. The leaves are silvery and lance-shaped and the plants grow to around 24 in (60 cm) high and 18 in (45 cm) wide. The **Mixed**

Useful Tip

Invest in a simple pH kit and find out if your soil is suitable for the plants you wish to grow: most plants like a slightly acidic (pH 5.5-6.5) soil.

Xeranthemum annuum Mixed Hybrids

Hybrids include singles and doubles in shades of pink, purple, mauve, red or white. This is an excellent cut flower.

ZONES 7–10.

Zinnia elegans

ZINNIA

Zinnia

This genus, found throughout Mexico and Central and South America, consists of 20 species of erect to spreading annuals, perennials and subshrubs. Some species are grown for cut flowers and mixed borders; shorter cultivars are good for edging or for containers. They bear daisy-like, terminal flowerheads in many colors including white, yellow, orange, red, purple and lilac.

CULTIVATION Marginally frost hardy, these plants do best in a sunny position in fertile, well-drained soil. Deadhead frequently. Propagate from seed sown under glass early in spring, or *in situ* in late spring.

Zinnia elegans
Youth-and-old-age

An upright, bushy Mexican annual, this is the best known of the zinnias. The wild form has purple flowerheads from summer to fall (autumn) and it grows fairly rapidly to 24-30 in (60–75 cm), with a smaller spread. The blooms of garden forms are up to 6 in (15 cm) across and come in white, red, pink, yellow, violet, orange or crimson. Cultivars include **'Envy'** (pale green semi-double blooms); the compact **Dreamland Series**, to which **'Dreamland Ivy'** (pale greenish yellow blooms) belongs; and the 6 in (15 cm) high **Thumbelina Series**, with 2 in (5 cm) wide flowerheads.

ZONES 8–11.

Useful Tip

Sow Zinnia seeds at intervals, starting in late spring, for a prolonged late-summer, early fall (autumn) display.

HARDINESS ZONE MAPS

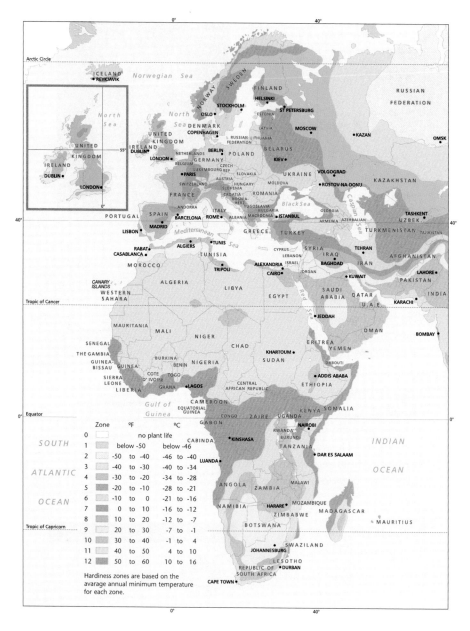

Zone	°F	°C
0	no plant life	
1	below -50	below -46
2	-50 to -40	-46 to -40
3	-40 to -30	-40 to -34
4	-30 to -20	-34 to -28
5	-20 to -10	-28 to -21
6	-10 to 0	-21 to -16
7	0 to 10	-16 to -12
8	10 to 20	-12 to -7
9	20 to 30	-7 to -1
10	30 to 40	-1 to 4
11	40 to 50	4 to 10
12	50 to 60	10 to 16

Hardiness zones are based on the avarage annual minimum temperature for each zone.

Note: The scale of this map differs from that of the following two maps.

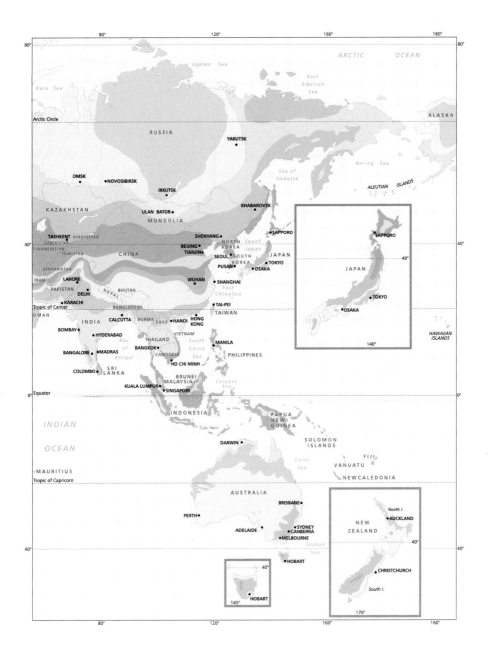

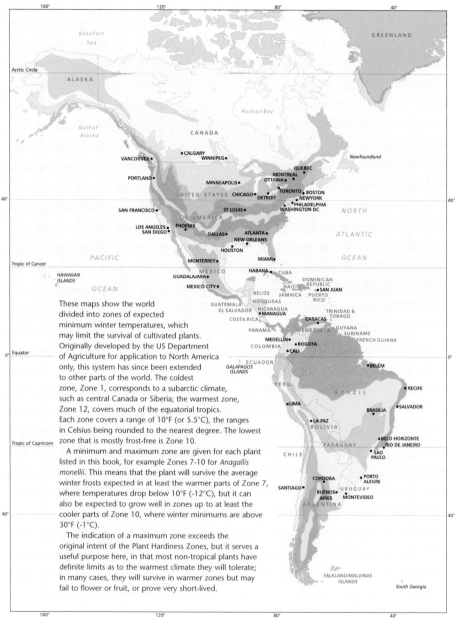

These maps show the world divided into zones of expected minimum winter temperatures, which may limit the survival of cultivated plants. Originally developed by the US Department of Agriculture for application to North America only, this system has since been extended to other parts of the world. The coldest zone, Zone 1, corresponds to a subarctic climate, such as central Canada or Siberia; the warmest zone, Zone 12, covers much of the equatorial tropics. Each zone covers a range of 10°F (or 5.5°C), the ranges in Celsius being rounded to the nearest degree. The lowest zone that is mostly frost-free is Zone 10.

A minimum and maximum zone are given for each plant listed in this book, for example Zones 7-10 for *Anagallis monellii*. This means that the plant will survive the average winter frosts expected in at least the warmer parts of Zone 7, where temperatures drop below 10°F (-12°C), but it can also be expected to grow well in zones up to at least the cooler parts of Zone 10, where winter minimums are above 30°F (-1°C).

The indication of a maximum zone exceeds the original intent of the Plant Hardiness Zones, but it serves a useful purpose here, in that most non-tropical plants have definite limits as to the warmest climate they will tolerate; in many cases, they will survive in warmer zones but may fail to flower or fruit, or prove very short-lived.

INDEX